LIKELY STORIES™

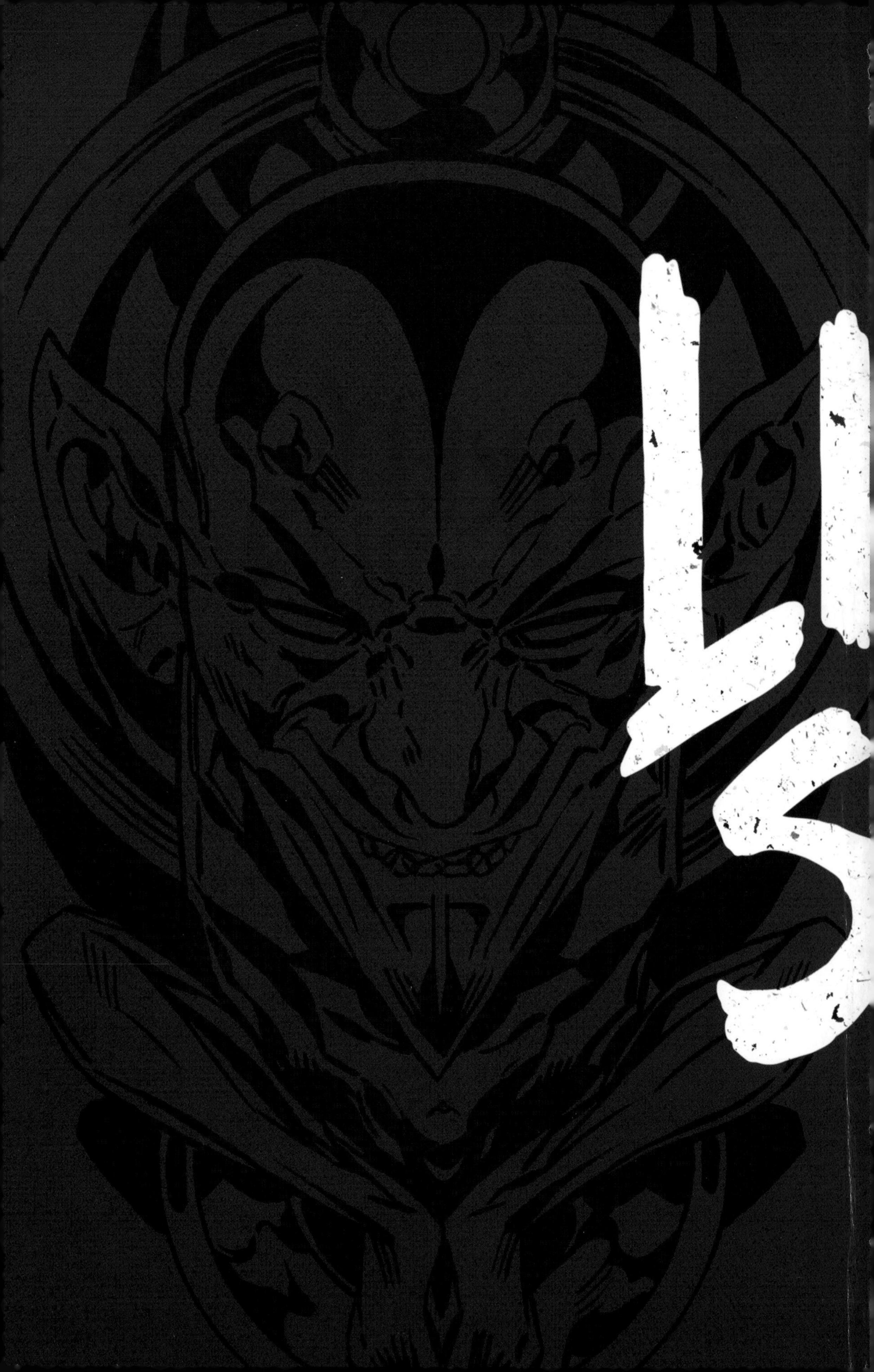

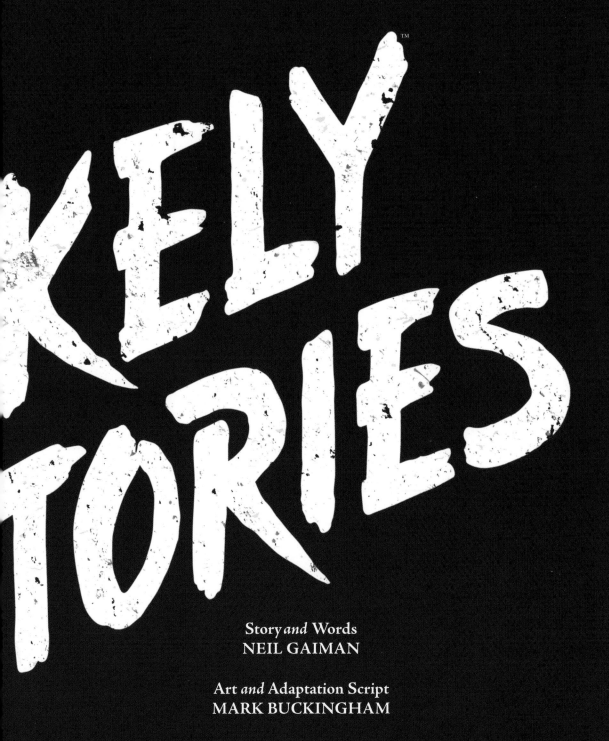

KELY
TORIES

Story *and* Words
NEIL GAIMAN

Art *and* Adaptation Script
MARK BUCKINGHAM

Colors
CHRIS BLYTHE

Letters
NATE PIEKOS *of* BLAMBOT®

Dark Horse Books

President and Publisher
MIKE RICHARDSON

Editor
DANIEL CHABON

Assistant Editor
BRETT ISRAEL

Designer
PATRICK SATTERFIELD

Digital Art Technicians
CHRISTINA McKENZIE & ADAM PRUETT

Published by Dark Horse Books
A division of Dark Horse Comics, Inc.
10956 SE Main Street
Milwaukie, OR 97222

DarkHorse.com

To find a comic shop in your area, check out the Comic Shop Locator Service: comicshoplocator.com

Library of Congress Cataloging-in-Publication Data

Names: Gaiman, Neil, author. | Buckingham, Mark, artist. | Blythe, Chris,
colourist. | Piekos, Nate, letterer.
Title: Likely stories / Neil Gaiman, story and words ; Mark Buckingham, art
and adaptation script ; Chris Blythe, colors ; Nate Piekos of Blambot,
letters.
Description: First edition. | Milwaukie, OR : Dark Horse Books, August 2018.
Identifiers: LCCN 2018013760 | ISBN 9781506705309 (hardback)
Subjects: LCSH: Comic books, strips, etc. | BISAC: COMICS & GRAPHIC NOVELS /
Fantasy. | COMICS & GRAPHIC NOVELS / Horror. | COMICS & GRAPHIC NOVELS /
Media Tie-In.
Classification: LCC PN6737.G3 A6 2018 | DDC 741.5/942--dc23
LC record available at https://lccn.loc.gov/2018013760

First edition: August 2018
ISBN 978-1-50670-530-9

10 9 8 7 6 5 4 3 2 1
Printed in China

NEIL HANKERSON Executive Vice President • TOM WEDDLE Chief Financial Officer • RANDY STRADLEY Vice President of
Publishing • NICK McWHORTER Chief Business Development Officer • MATT PARKINSON Vice President of Marketing • DALE
LaFOUNTAIN Vice President of Information Technology • CARA NIECE Vice President of Production and Scheduling • MARK
BERNARDI Vice President of Book Trade and Digital Sales • KEN LIZZI General Counsel • DAVE MARSHALL Editor in Chief
DAVEY ESTRADA Editorial Director • CHRIS WARNER Senior Books Editor • CARY GRAZZINI Director of Specialty Projects
LIA RIBACCHI Art Director • VANESSA TODD-HOLMES Director of Print Purchasing • MATT DRYER Director of Digital Art
and Prepress • MICHAEL GOMBOS Director of International Publishing and Licensing • KARI YADRO Director of Custom Programs

PROLOGUE

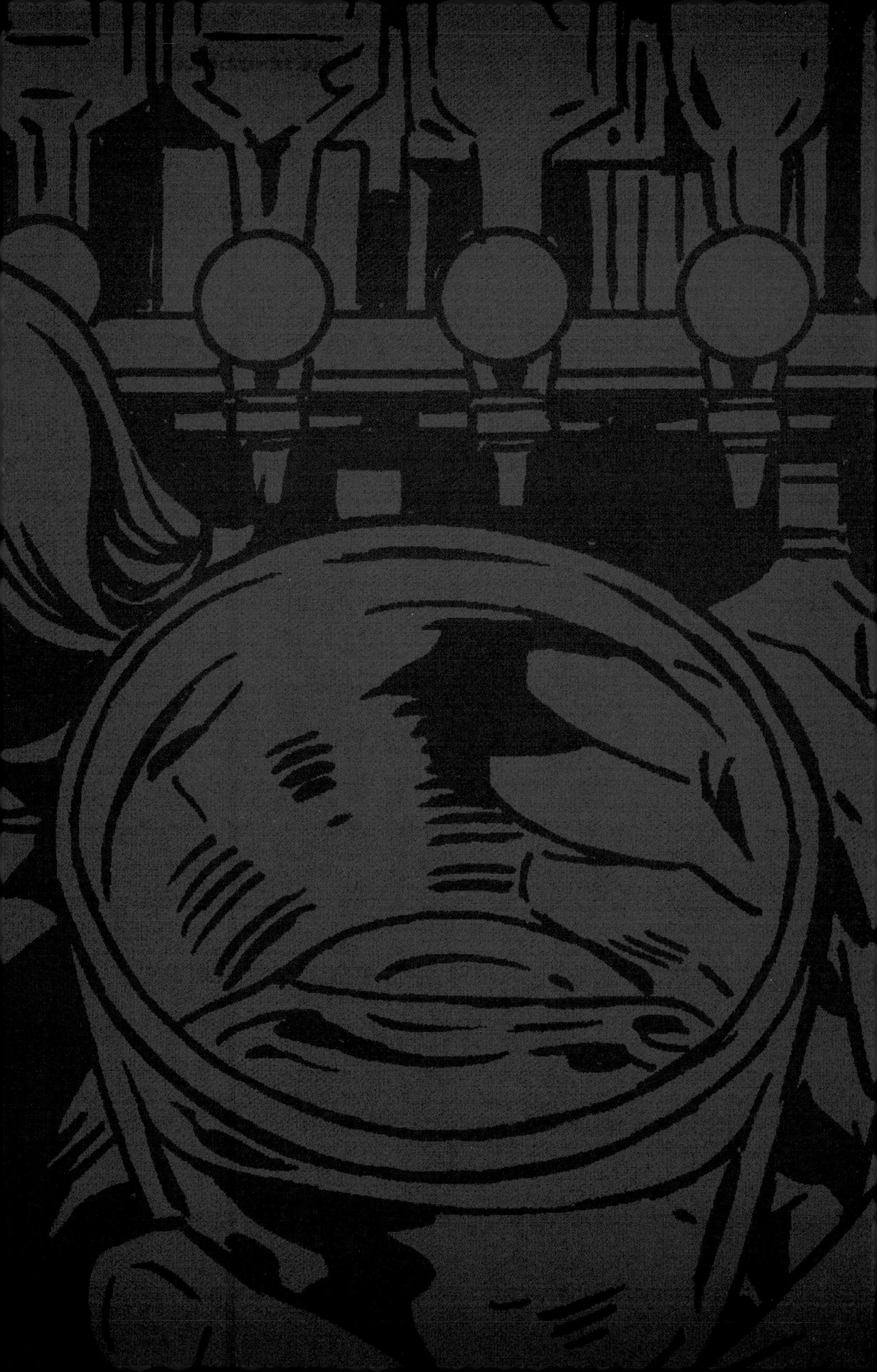

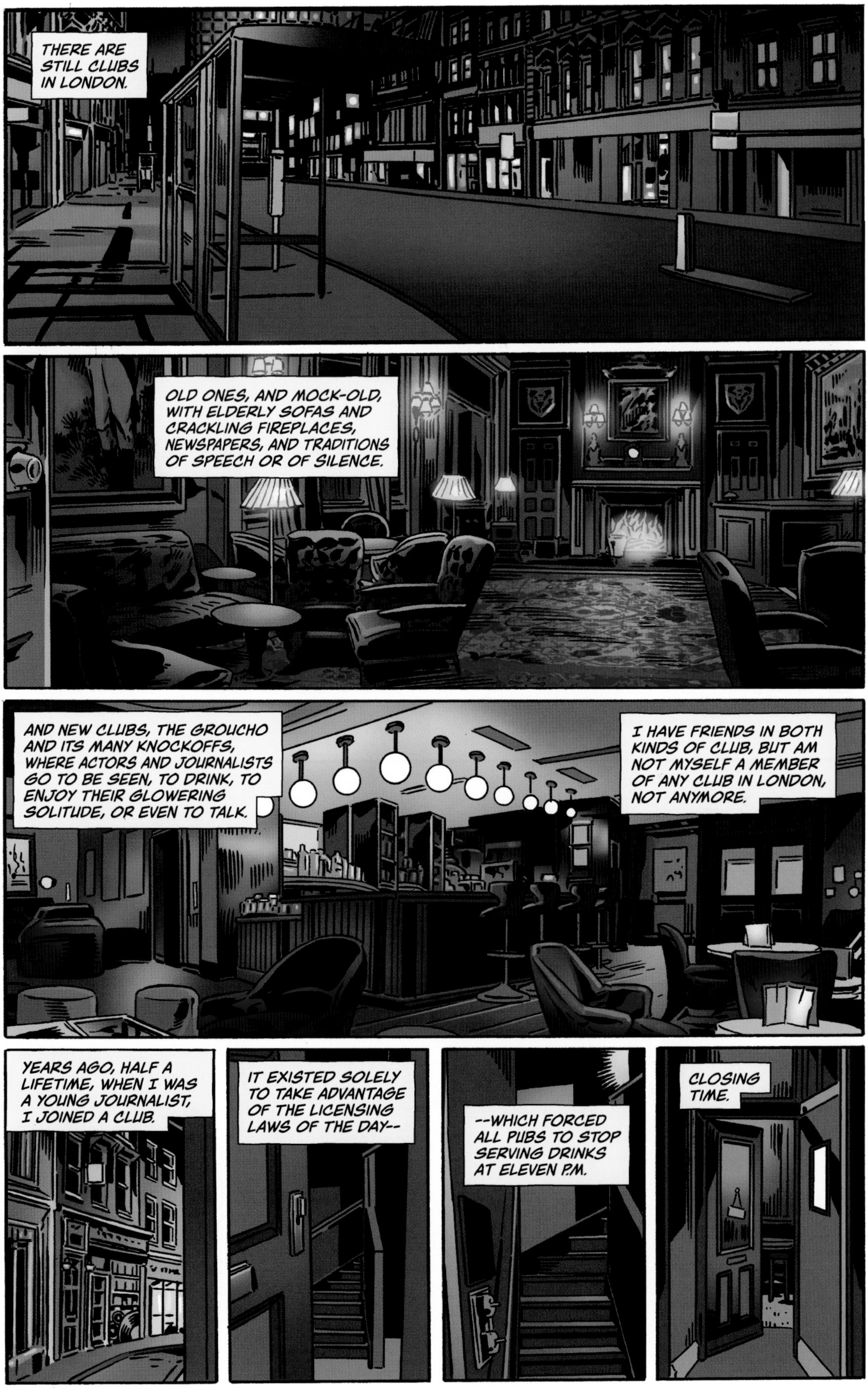
THERE ARE STILL CLUBS IN LONDON.
OLD ONES, AND MOCK-OLD, WITH ELDERLY SOFAS AND CRACKLING FIREPLACES, NEWSPAPERS, AND TRADITIONS OF SPEECH OR OF SILENCE.
AND NEW CLUBS, THE GROUCHO AND ITS MANY KNOCKOFFS, WHERE ACTORS AND JOURNALISTS GO TO BE SEEN, TO DRINK, TO ENJOY THEIR GLOWERING SOLITUDE, OR EVEN TO TALK.
I HAVE FRIENDS IN BOTH KINDS OF CLUB, BUT AM NOT MYSELF A MEMBER OF ANY CLUB IN LONDON, NOT ANYMORE.
YEARS AGO, HALF A LIFETIME, WHEN I WAS A YOUNG JOURNALIST, I JOINED A CLUB.
IT EXISTED SOLELY TO TAKE ADVANTAGE OF THE LICENSING LAWS OF THE DAY--
--WHICH FORCED ALL PUBS TO STOP SERVING DRINKS AT ELEVEN P.M.
CLOSING TIME.

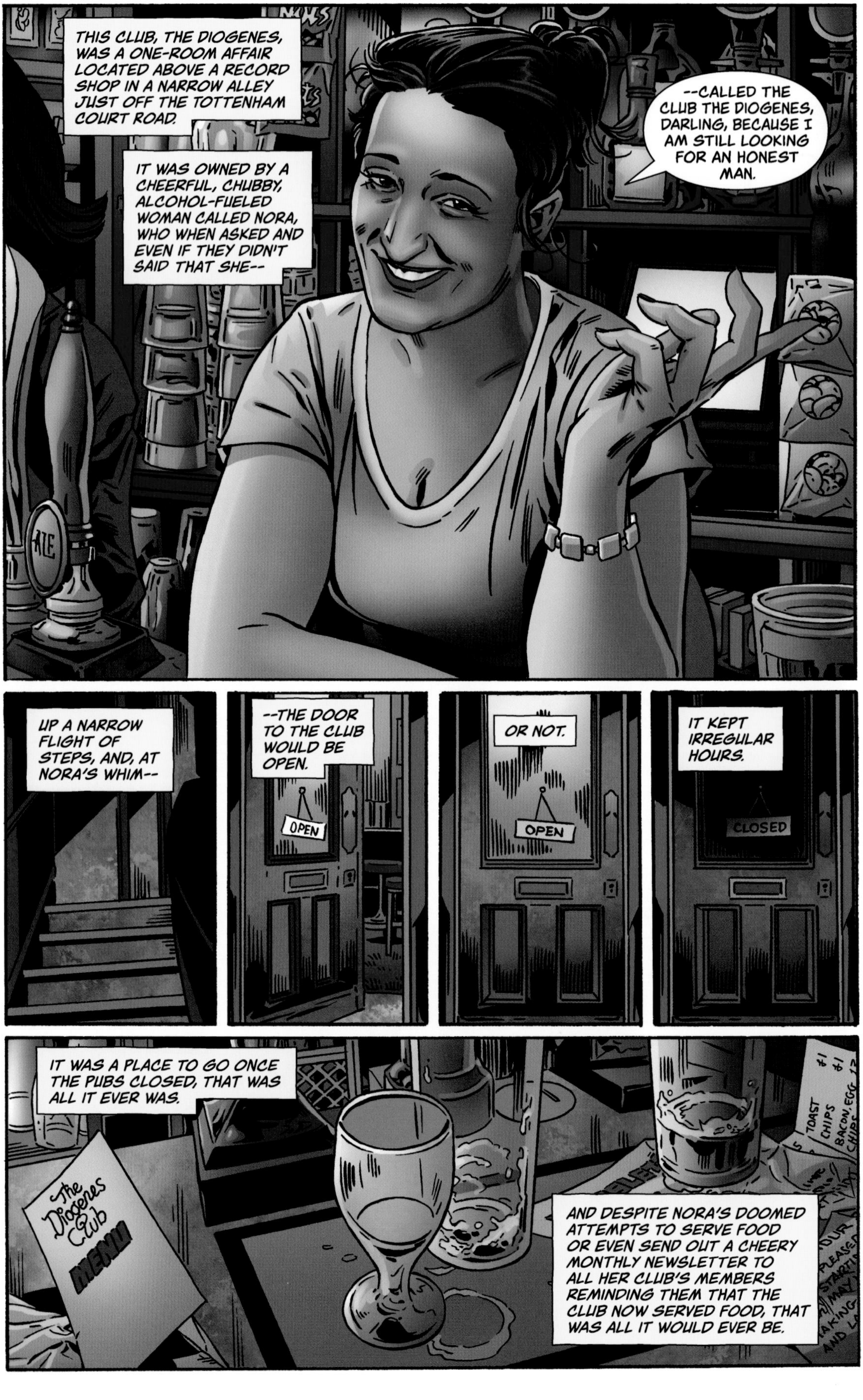
THIS CLUB, THE DIOGENES, WAS A ONE-ROOM AFFAIR LOCATED ABOVE A RECORD SHOP IN A NARROW ALLEY JUST OFF THE TOTTENHAM COURT ROAD.
IT WAS OWNED BY A CHEERFUL, CHUBBY, ALCOHOL-FUELED WOMAN CALLED NORA, WHO WHEN ASKED AND EVEN IF THEY DIDN'T SAID THAT SHE--
--CALLED THE CLUB THE DIOGENES, DARLING, BECAUSE I AM STILL LOOKING FOR AN HONEST MAN.
ALE
UP A NARROW FLIGHT OF STEPS, AND, AT NORA'S WHIM--
--THE DOOR TO THE CLUB WOULD BE OPEN.
OPEN
OR NOT.
OPEN
IT KEPT IRREGULAR HOURS.
CLOSED
IT WAS A PLACE TO GO ONCE THE PUBS CLOSED, THAT WAS ALL IT EVER WAS.
The Diogenes Club
MENU
TOAST
CHIPS
BACON, EGG
AND DESPITE NORA'S DOOMED ATTEMPTS TO SERVE FOOD OR EVEN SEND OUT A CHEERY MONTHLY NEWSLETTER TO ALL HER CLUB'S MEMBERS REMINDING THEM THAT THE CLUB NOW SERVED FOOD, THAT WAS ALL IT WOULD EVER BE.

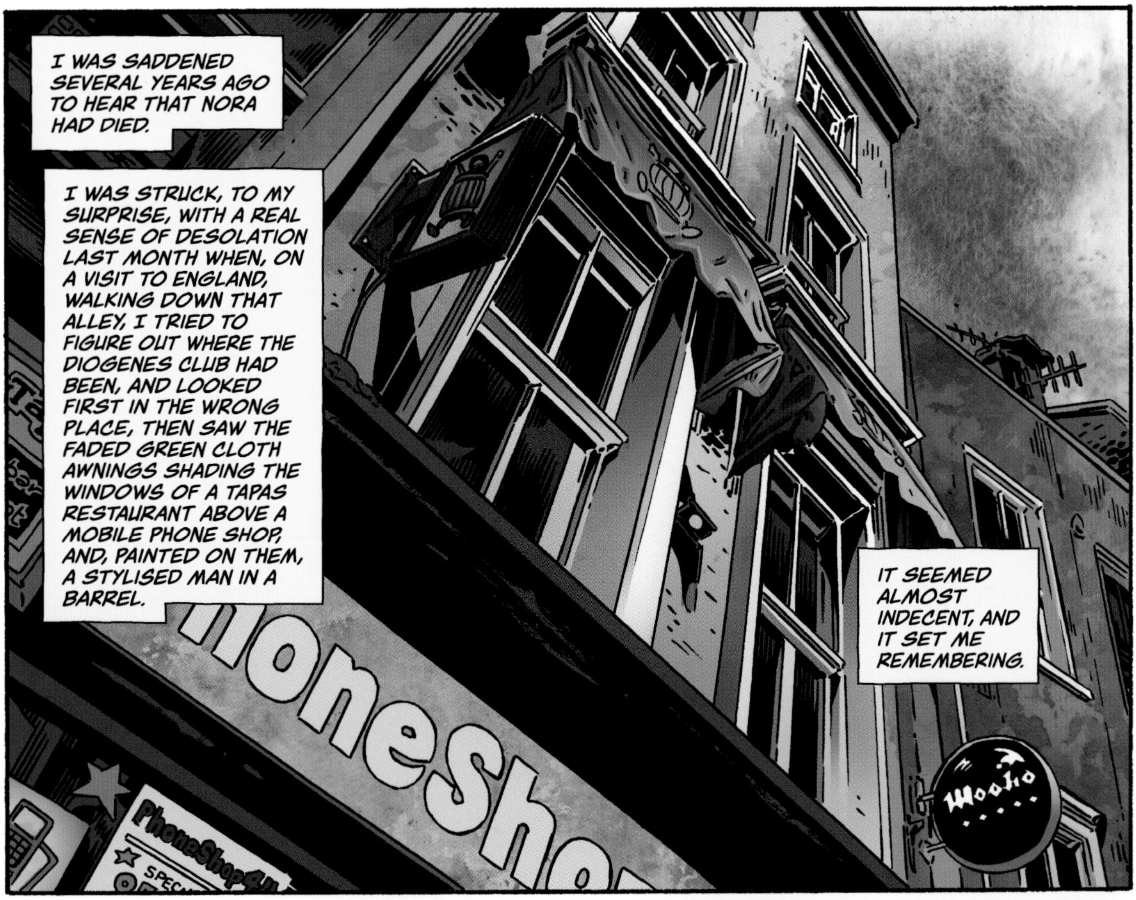
I WAS SADDENED SEVERAL YEARS AGO TO HEAR THAT NORA HAD DIED.
I WAS STRUCK, TO MY SURPRISE, WITH A REAL SENSE OF DESOLATION LAST MONTH WHEN, ON A VISIT TO ENGLAND, WALKING DOWN THAT ALLEY, I TRIED TO FIGURE OUT WHERE THE DIOGENES CLUB HAD BEEN, AND LOOKED FIRST IN THE WRONG PLACE, THEN SAW THE FADED GREEN CLOTH AWNINGS SHADING THE WINDOWS OF A TAPAS RESTAURANT ABOVE A MOBILE PHONE SHOP, AND, PAINTED ON THEM, A STYLISED MAN IN A BARREL.
IT SEEMED ALMOST INDECENT, AND IT SET ME REMEMBERING.
honeSho
PhoneShop

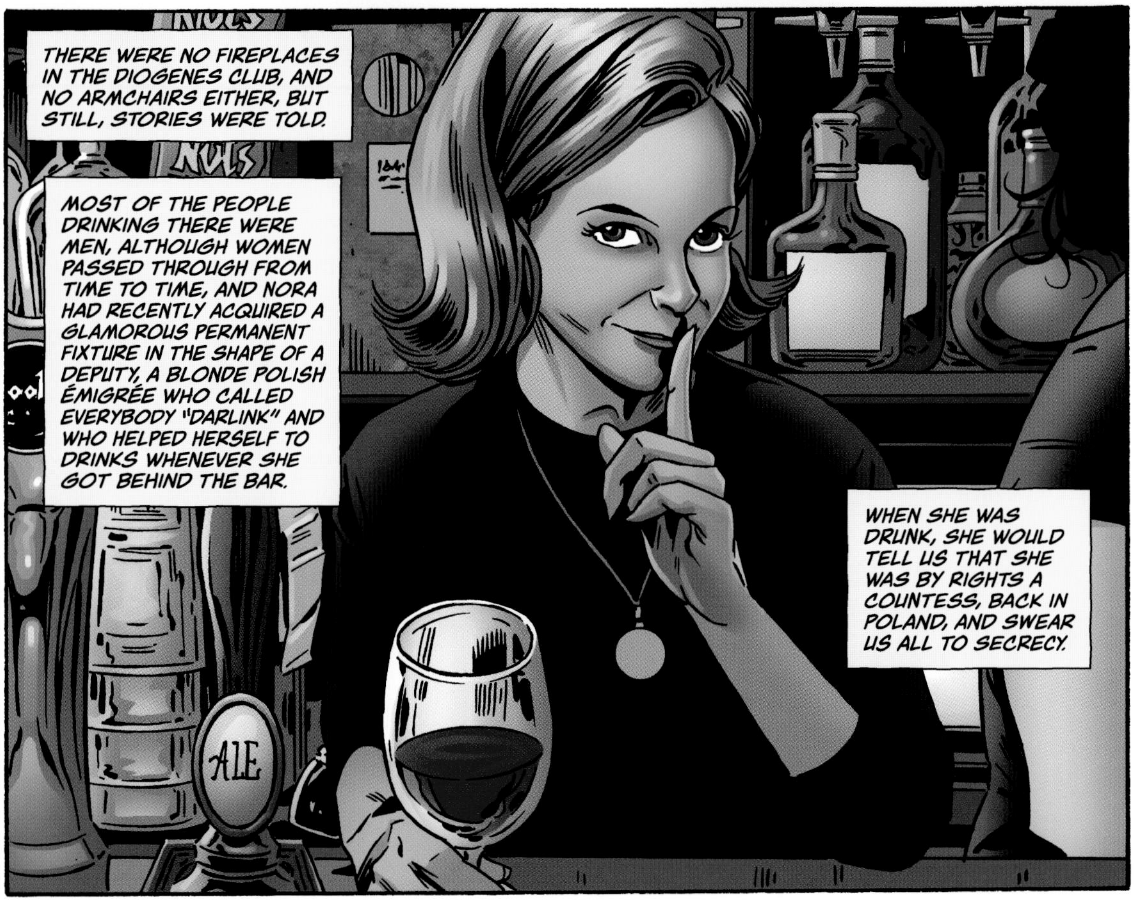
THERE WERE NO FIREPLACES IN THE DIOGENES CLUB, AND NO ARMCHAIRS EITHER, BUT STILL, STORIES WERE TOLD.
MOST OF THE PEOPLE DRINKING THERE WERE MEN, ALTHOUGH WOMEN PASSED THROUGH FROM TIME TO TIME, AND NORA HAD RECENTLY ACQUIRED A GLAMOROUS PERMANENT FIXTURE IN THE SHAPE OF A DEPUTY, A BLONDE POLISH ÉMIGRÉE WHO CALLED EVERYBODY "DARLINK" AND WHO HELPED HERSELF TO DRINKS WHENEVER SHE GOT BEHIND THE BAR.
WHEN SHE WAS DRUNK, SHE WOULD TELL US THAT SHE WAS BY RIGHTS A COUNTESS, BACK IN POLAND, AND SWEAR US ALL TO SECRECY.
NUTS
ALE

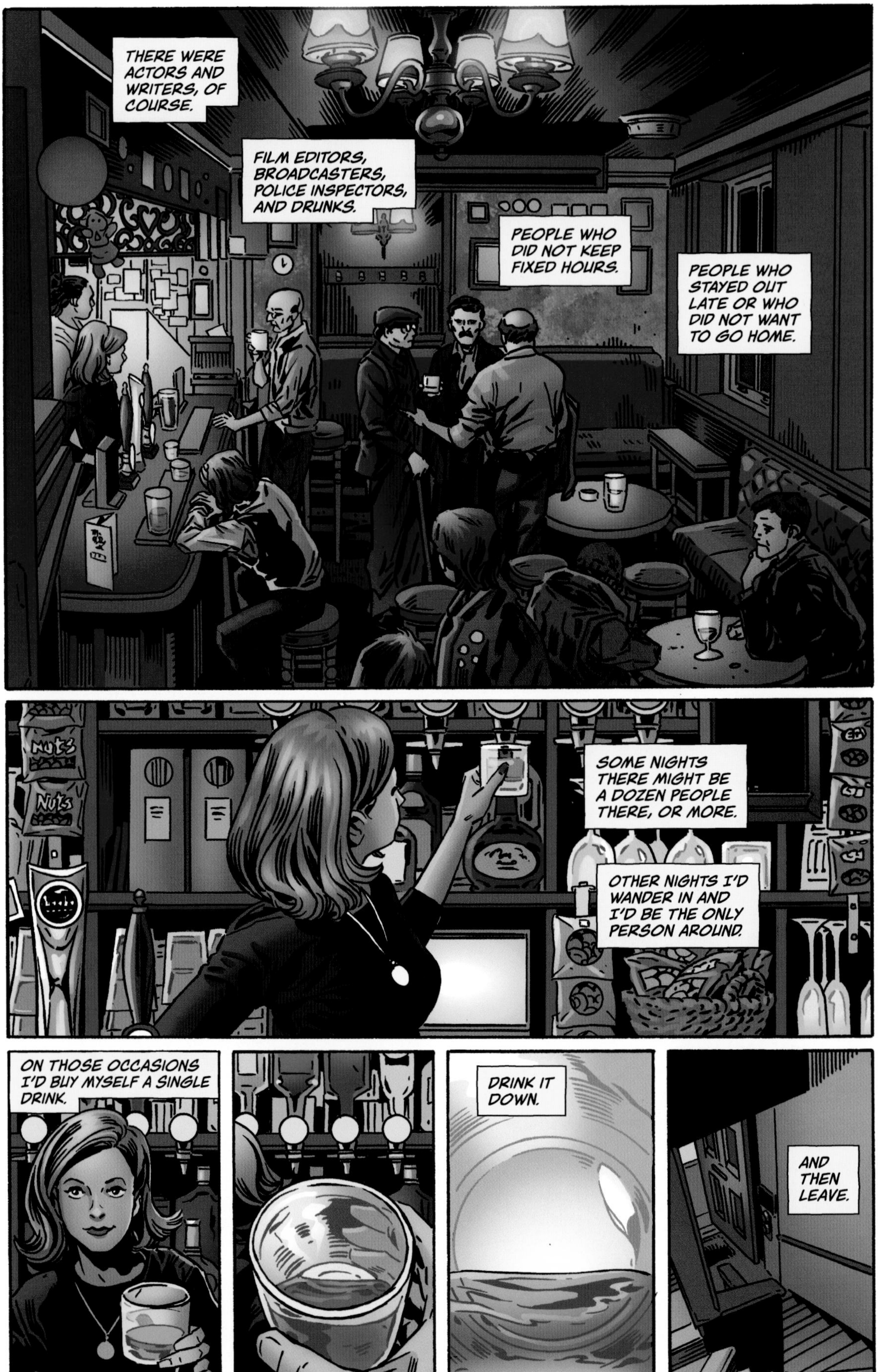
THERE WERE ACTORS AND WRITERS, OF COURSE.
FILM EDITORS, BROADCASTERS, POLICE INSPECTORS, AND DRUNKS.
PEOPLE WHO DID NOT KEEP FIXED HOURS.
PEOPLE WHO STAYED OUT LATE OR WHO DID NOT WANT TO GO HOME.
NUTS
NUTS
SOME NIGHTS THERE MIGHT BE A DOZEN PEOPLE THERE, OR MORE.
OTHER NIGHTS I'D WANDER IN AND I'D BE THE ONLY PERSON AROUND.
ON THOSE OCCASIONS I'D BUY MYSELF A SINGLE DRINK.
DRINK IT DOWN.
AND THEN LEAVE.

FOREIGN
PARTS

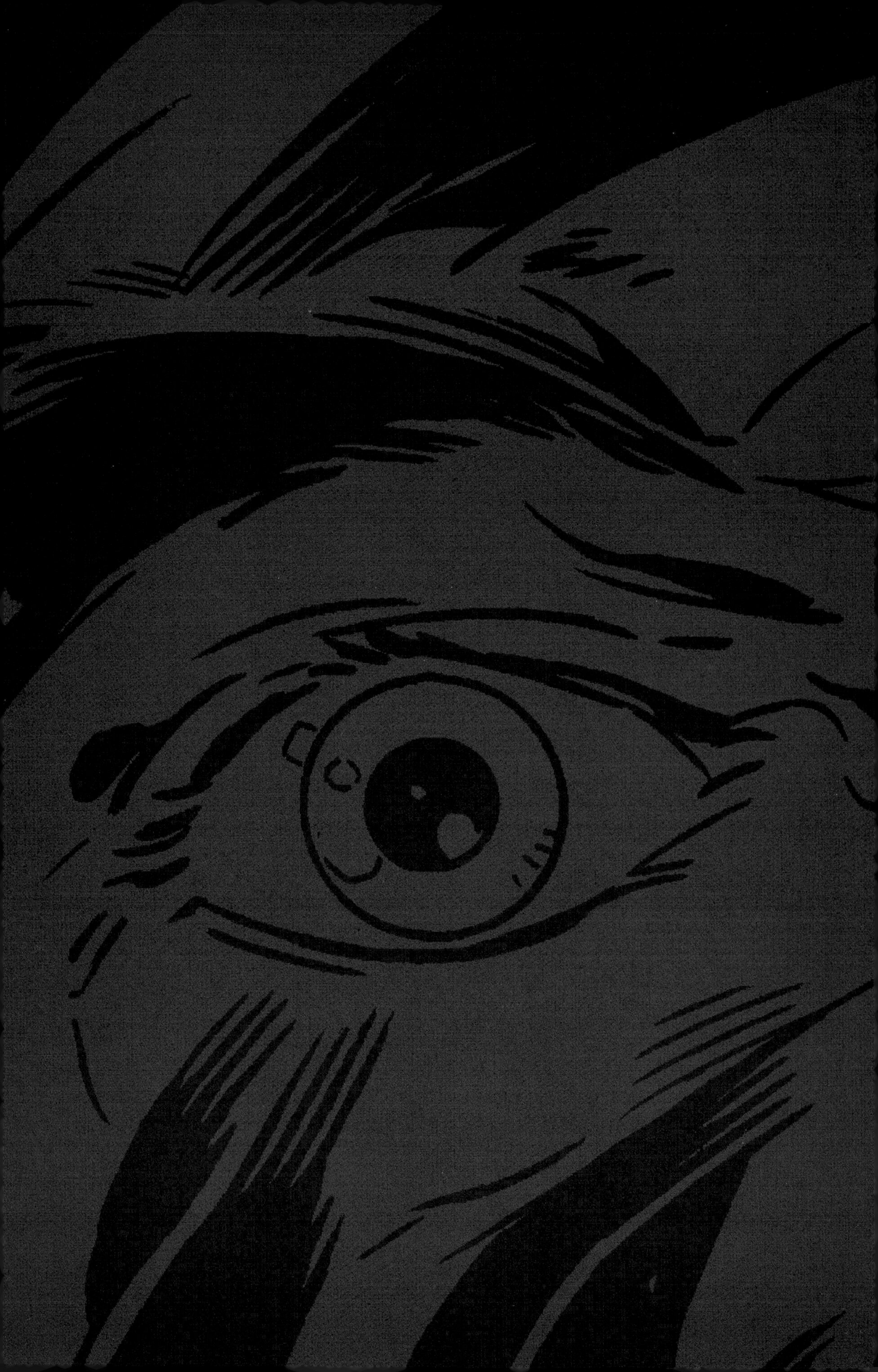

SIMON POWERS DIDN'T LIKE SEX. NOT REALLY.

HE DISLIKED HAVING SOMEONE ELSE IN THE SAME BED AS HIMSELF.

HE SUSPECTED THAT HE CAME TOO SOON.

HE ALWAYS FELT UNCOMFORTABLY THAT HIS PERFORMANCE WAS IN SOME WAY BEING GRADED...

...LIKE A DRIVING TEST OR A PRACTICAL EXAMINATION.

HE HAD GOT LAID IN COLLEGE A FEW TIMES AND ONCE, THREE YEARS AGO, AFTER THE OFFICE NEW YEAR'S PARTY.

BUT THAT HAD BEEN THAT, AND AS FAR AS SIMON WAS CONCERNED, HE WAS WELL OUT OF IT.

IT OCCURRED TO HIM ONCE, DURING A SLACK TIME AT THE OFFICE, THAT HE WOULD HAVE LIKED TO HAVE LIVED IN THE DAYS OF QUEEN VICTORIA...

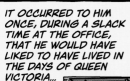

...WHERE WELL-BROUGHT UP WOMEN WERE NO MORE THAN RESENTFUL SEX DOLLS IN THE BEDROOM.

THEY'D UNLACE THEIR STAYS, LOOSEN THEIR PETTICOATS (REVEALING PINKISH-WHITE FLESH)...

...THEN LIE BACK AND SUFFER THE INDIGNITIES OF THE CARNAL ACT.

AN INDIGNITY IT WOULD NEVER EVEN OCCUR TO THEM THAT THEY WERE MEANT TO ENJOY.

HE FILED IT AWAY FOR LATER, ANOTHER MASTURBATORY FANTASY.

SIMON MASTURBATED A GREAT DEAL.

EVERY NIGHT.

SOMETIMES MORE THAN THAT IF HE WAS UNABLE TO SLEEP.

HE COULD TAKE AS LONG, OR AS SHORT, A TIME TO CLIMAX AS HE WISHED.

AND IN HIS MIND HE HAD THEM ALL.

FILM AND TELEVISION STARS.

WOMEN FROM THE OFFICE.

SCHOOL GIRLS.

THE NAKED MODELS WHO POUTED FROM THE CRUMPLED PAGES OF FIESTA.

FACELESS SLAVES IN CHAINS.

TANNED BOYS WITH BODIES LIKE GREEK GODS.

NIGHT AFTER NIGHT THEY PARADED IN FRONT OF HIM.

IT WAS SAFER THAT WAY.

IN HIS MIND.

AND AFTERWARD HE'D FALL ASLEEP, COMFORTABLE AND SAFE IN A WORLD HE CONTROLLED, AND HE'D SLEEP WITHOUT DREAMING.

OR AT LEAST, HE NEVER REMEMBERED HIS DREAMS IN THE MORNING.

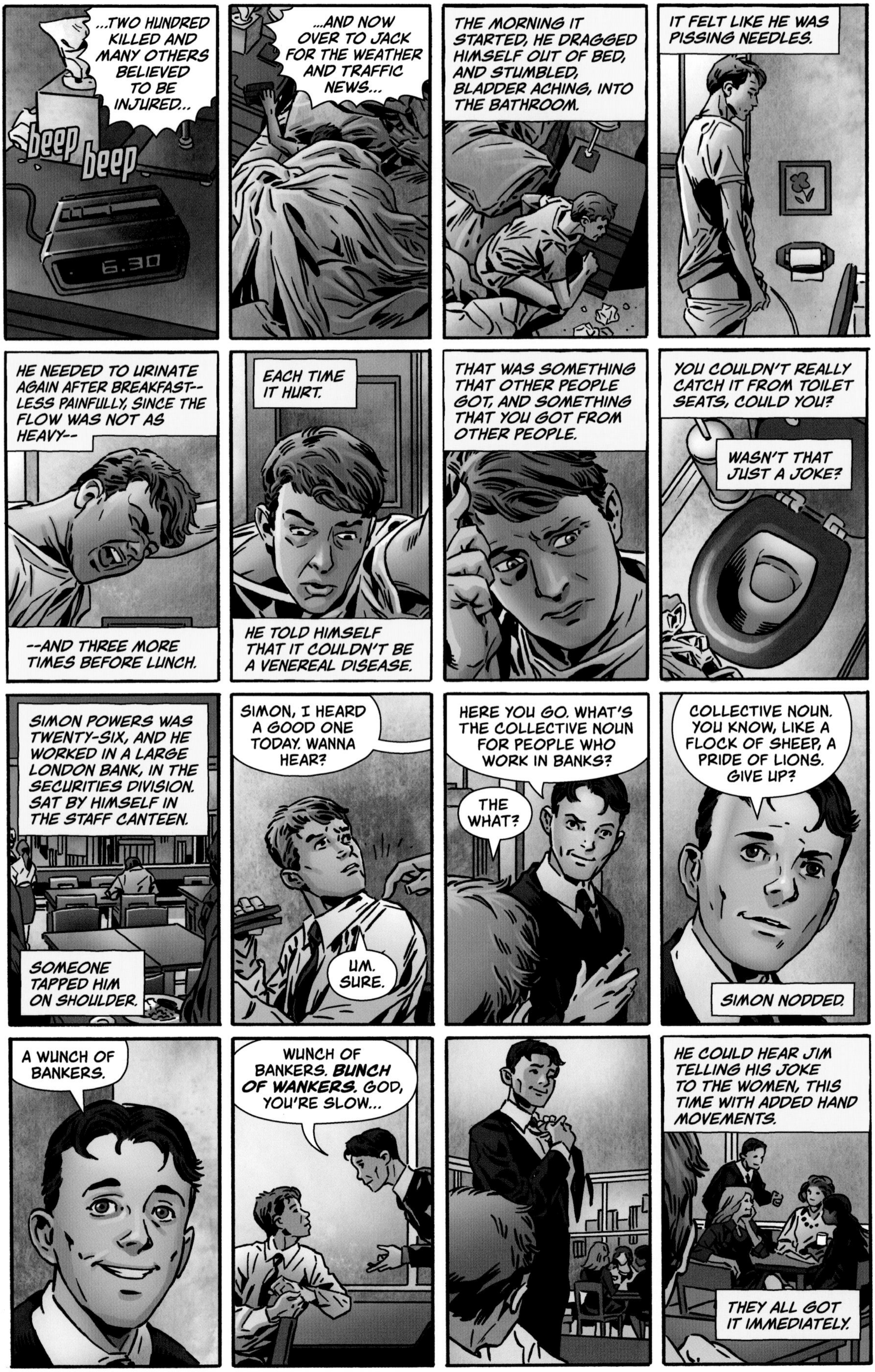
...TWO HUNDRED KILLED AND MANY OTHERS BELIEVED TO BE INJURED...
beep beep
6.30
...AND NOW OVER TO JACK FOR THE WEATHER AND TRAFFIC NEWS...
THE MORNING IT STARTED, HE DRAGGED HIMSELF OUT OF BED, AND STUMBLED, BLADDER ACHING, INTO THE BATHROOM.
IT FELT LIKE HE WAS PISSING NEEDLES.
HE NEEDED TO URINATE AGAIN AFTER BREAKFAST--LESS PAINFULLY, SINCE THE FLOW WAS NOT AS HEAVY--
--AND THREE MORE TIMES BEFORE LUNCH.
EACH TIME IT HURT.
HE TOLD HIMSELF THAT IT COULDN'T BE A VENEREAL DISEASE.
THAT WAS SOMETHING THAT OTHER PEOPLE GOT, AND SOMETHING THAT YOU GOT FROM OTHER PEOPLE.
YOU COULDN'T REALLY CATCH IT FROM TOILET SEATS, COULD YOU?
WASN'T THAT JUST A JOKE?
SIMON POWERS WAS TWENTY-SIX, AND HE WORKED IN A LARGE LONDON BANK, IN THE SECURITIES DIVISION. SAT BY HIMSELF IN THE STAFF CANTEEN.
SOMEONE TAPPED HIM ON SHOULDER.
SIMON, I HEARD A GOOD ONE TODAY. WANNA HEAR?
UM. SURE.
HERE YOU GO. WHAT'S THE COLLECTIVE NOUN FOR PEOPLE WHO WORK IN BANKS?
THE WHAT?
COLLECTIVE NOUN. YOU KNOW, LIKE A FLOCK OF SHEEP, A PRIDE OF LIONS. GIVE UP?
SIMON NODDED.
A WUNCH OF BANKERS.
WUNCH OF BANKERS. BUNCH OF WANKERS. GOD, YOU'RE SLOW...
HE COULD HEAR JIM TELLING HIS JOKE TO THE WOMEN, THIS TIME WITH ADDED HAND MOVEMENTS.
THEY ALL GOT IT IMMEDIATELY.

THAT NIGHT HE TRIED TO REMEMBER WHAT HE KNEW ABOUT VENEREAL DISEASES.

THERE WAS SYPHILIS, WHICH POCKED YOUR FACE AND DROVE THE KINGS OF ENGLAND MAD.

GONORRHEA-- THE CLAP--A GREEN OOZING AND MORE MADNESS.

CRABS, LITTLE PUBIC LICE, WHICH NESTED AND ITCHED.

HE INSPECTED HIS PUBIC HAIRS THROUGH A MAGNIFYING GLASS, BUT NOTHING MOVED.

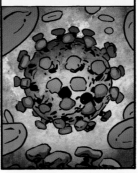

AIDS, THE EIGHTIES PLAGUE, A PLEA FOR CLEAN NEEDLES AND SAFER SEXUAL HABITS.

BUT WHAT COULD BE SAFER THAN A CLEAN WANK FOR ONE INTO A FRESH HANDFUL OF WHITE TISSUES?

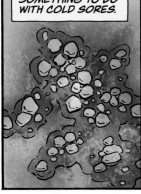

HERPES, WHICH HAD SOMETHING TO DO WITH COLD SORES.

HE CHECKED HIS LIPS IN THE MIRROR, THEY LOOKED FINE.

THAT WAS ALL HE KNEW.

AND HE WENT TO BED AND FRETTED HIMSELF TO SLEEP, WITHOUT DARING TO MASTURBATE.

SIMON DID NOTHING ABOUT THE PAIN FOR ANOTHER TWO DAYS.

HE HOPED IT WOULD GO AWAY, OR GET BETTER ON ITS OWN. IT DIDN'T. IT GOT WORSE.

THE PAIN CONTINUED FOR UP TO AN HOUR AFTER URINATION. HIS PENIS FELT RAW AND BRUISED INSIDE.

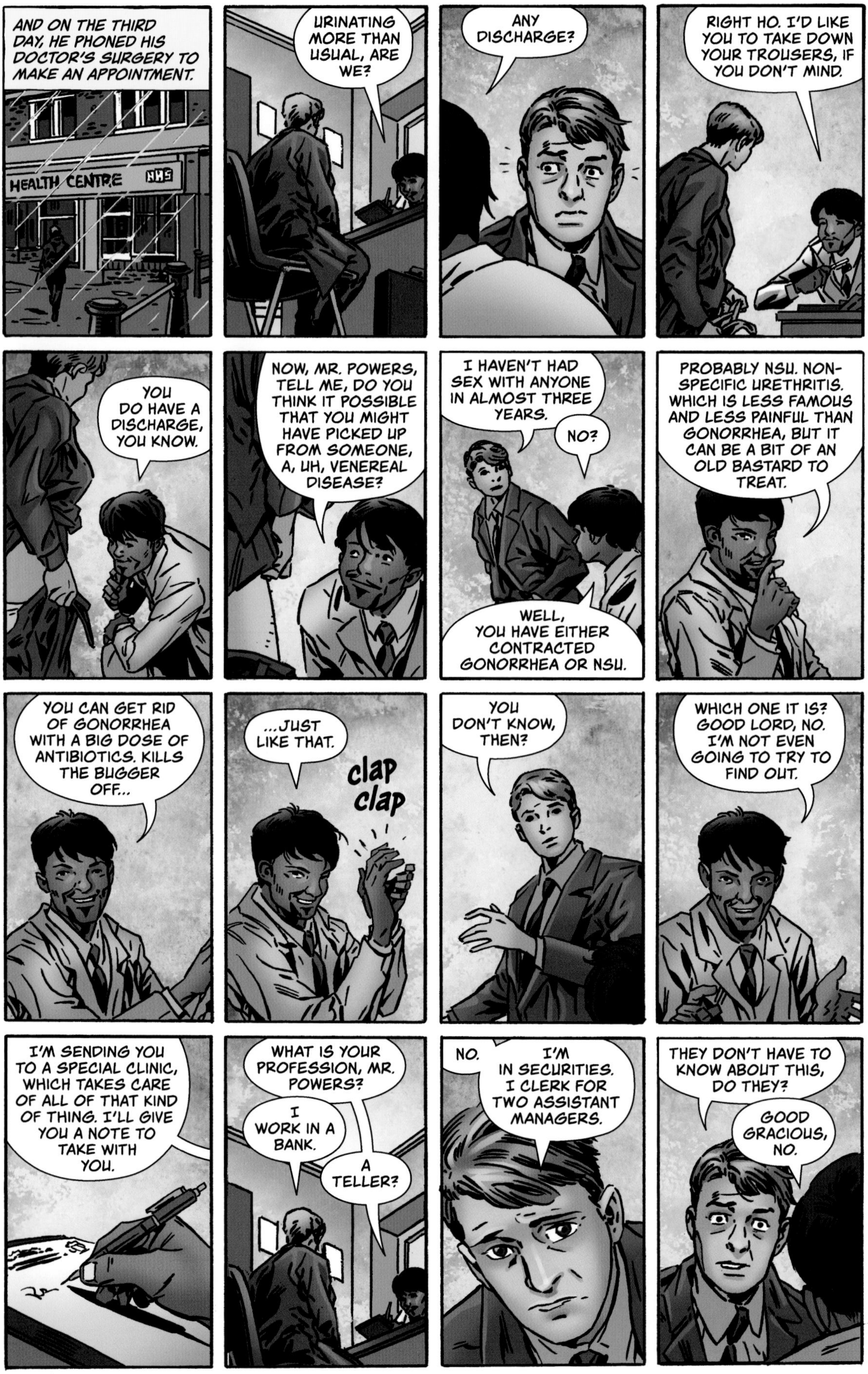
AND ON THE THIRD DAY, HE PHONED HIS DOCTOR'S SURGERY TO MAKE AN APPOINTMENT.
HEALTH CENTRE
NHS
URINATING MORE THAN USUAL, ARE WE?
ANY DISCHARGE?
RIGHT HO. I'D LIKE YOU TO TAKE DOWN YOUR TROUSERS, IF YOU DON'T MIND.
YOU DO HAVE A DISCHARGE, YOU KNOW.
NOW, MR. POWERS, TELL ME, DO YOU THINK IT POSSIBLE THAT YOU MIGHT HAVE PICKED UP FROM SOMEONE, A, UH, VENEREAL DISEASE?
I HAVEN'T HAD SEX WITH ANYONE IN ALMOST THREE YEARS.
NO?
WELL, YOU HAVE EITHER CONTRACTED GONORRHEA OR NSU.
PROBABLY NSU. NON-SPECIFIC URETHRITIS. WHICH IS LESS FAMOUS AND LESS PAINFUL THAN GONORRHEA, BUT IT CAN BE A BIT OF AN OLD BASTARD TO TREAT.
YOU CAN GET RID OF GONORRHEA WITH A BIG DOSE OF ANTIBIOTICS. KILLS THE BUGGER OFF...
...JUST LIKE THAT.
clap clap
YOU DON'T KNOW, THEN?
WHICH ONE IT IS? GOOD LORD, NO. I'M NOT EVEN GOING TO TRY TO FIND OUT.
I'M SENDING YOU TO A SPECIAL CLINIC, WHICH TAKES CARE OF ALL OF THAT KIND OF THING. I'LL GIVE YOU A NOTE TO TAKE WITH YOU.
WHAT IS YOUR PROFESSION, MR. POWERS?
I WORK IN A BANK.
A TELLER?
NO.
I'M IN SECURITIES. I CLERK FOR TWO ASSISTANT MANAGERS.
THEY DON'T HAVE TO KNOW ABOUT THIS, DO THEY?
GOOD GRACIOUS, NO.

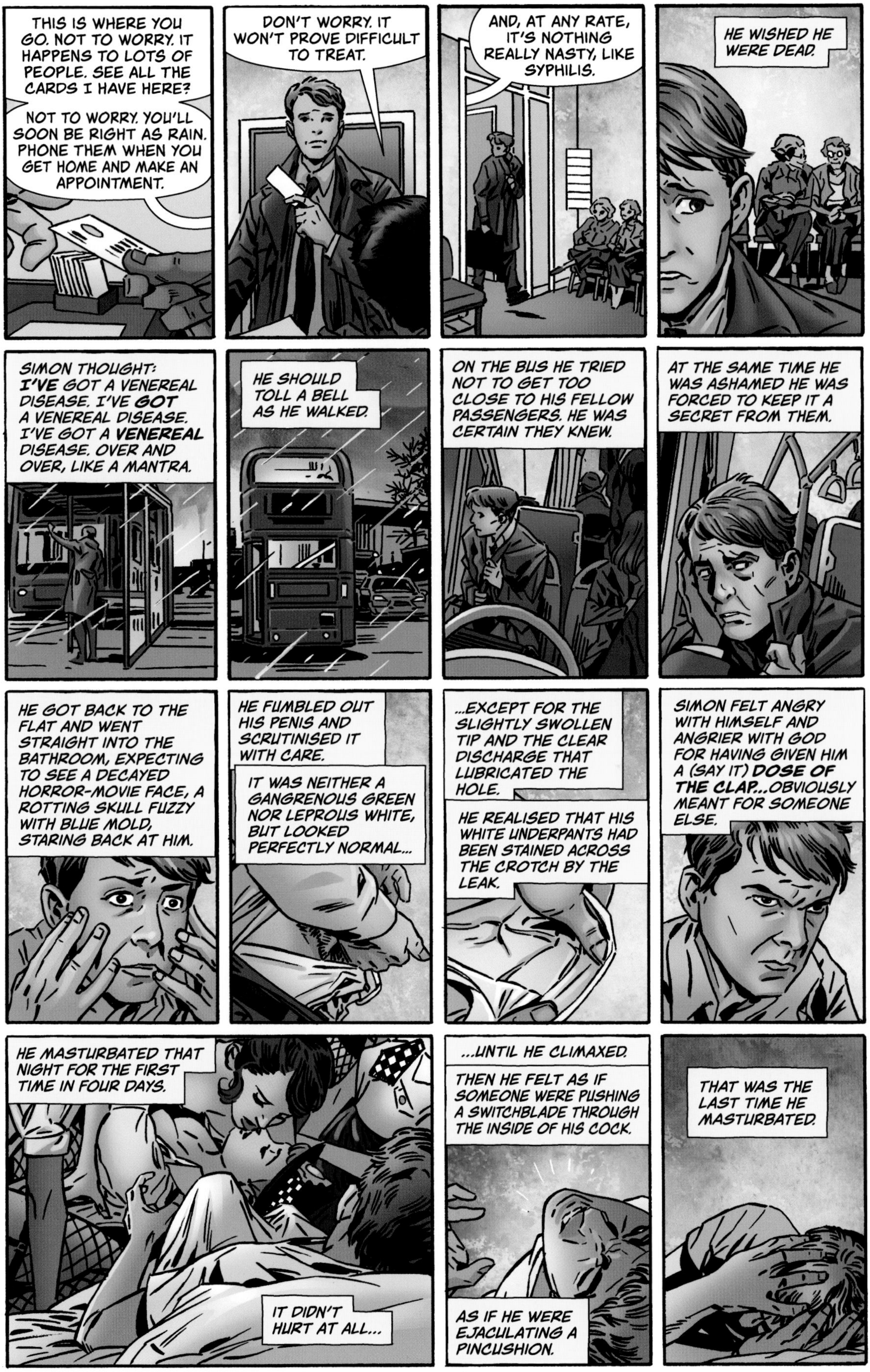
THIS IS WHERE YOU GO. NOT TO WORRY. IT HAPPENS TO LOTS OF PEOPLE. SEE ALL THE CARDS I HAVE HERE?
NOT TO WORRY. YOU'LL SOON BE RIGHT AS RAIN. PHONE THEM WHEN YOU GET HOME AND MAKE AN APPOINTMENT.
DON'T WORRY. IT WON'T PROVE DIFFICULT TO TREAT.
AND, AT ANY RATE, IT'S NOTHING REALLY NASTY, LIKE SYPHILIS.
HE WISHED HE WERE DEAD.
SIMON THOUGHT: I'VE GOT A VENEREAL DISEASE. I'VE GOT A VENEREAL DISEASE. I'VE GOT A VENEREAL DISEASE. OVER AND OVER, LIKE A MANTRA.
HE SHOULD TOLL A BELL AS HE WALKED.
ON THE BUS HE TRIED NOT TO GET TOO CLOSE TO HIS FELLOW PASSENGERS. HE WAS CERTAIN THEY KNEW.
AT THE SAME TIME HE WAS ASHAMED HE WAS FORCED TO KEEP IT A SECRET FROM THEM.
HE GOT BACK TO THE FLAT AND WENT STRAIGHT INTO THE BATHROOM, EXPECTING TO SEE A DECAYED HORROR-MOVIE FACE, A ROTTING SKULL FUZZY WITH BLUE MOLD, STARING BACK AT HIM.
HE FUMBLED OUT HIS PENIS AND SCRUTINISED IT WITH CARE.
IT WAS NEITHER A GANGRENOUS GREEN NOR LEPROUS WHITE, BUT LOOKED PERFECTLY NORMAL...
...EXCEPT FOR THE SLIGHTLY SWOLLEN TIP AND THE CLEAR DISCHARGE THAT LUBRICATED THE HOLE.
HE REALISED THAT HIS WHITE UNDERPANTS HAD BEEN STAINED ACROSS THE CROTCH BY THE LEAK.
SIMON FELT ANGRY WITH HIMSELF AND ANGRIER WITH GOD FOR HAVING GIVEN HIM A (SAY IT) DOSE OF THE CLAP...OBVIOUSLY MEANT FOR SOMEONE ELSE.
HE MASTURBATED THAT NIGHT FOR THE FIRST TIME IN FOUR DAYS.
IT DIDN'T HURT AT ALL...
...UNTIL HE CLIMAXED.
THEN HE FELT AS IF SOMEONE WERE PUSHING A SWITCHBLADE THROUGH THE INSIDE OF HIS COCK.
AS IF HE WERE EJACULATING A PINCUSHION.
THAT WAS THE LAST TIME HE MASTURBATED.

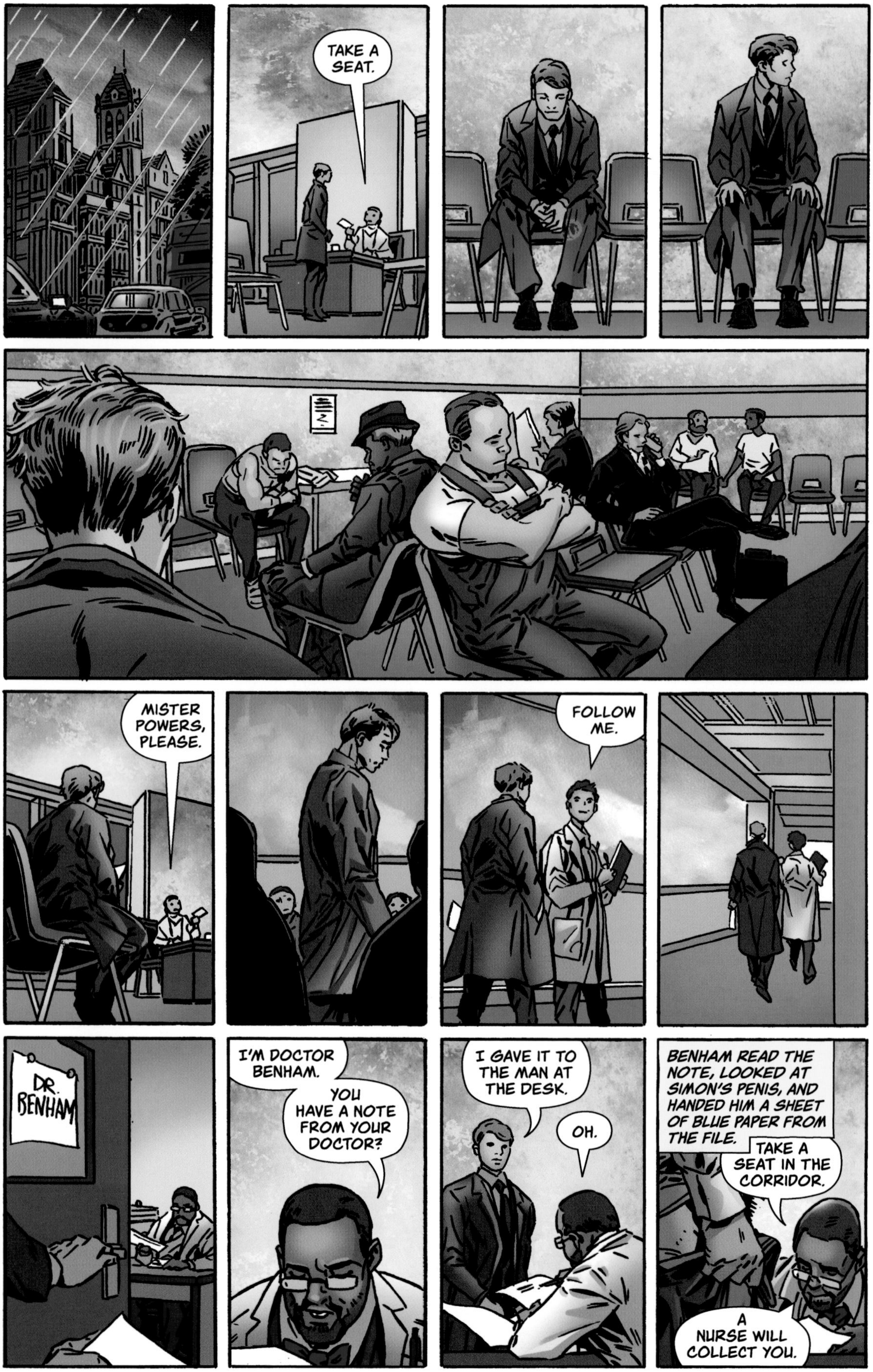
TAKE A SEAT.
MISTER POWERS, PLEASE.
FOLLOW ME.
DR. BENHAM
I'M DOCTOR BENHAM.
YOU HAVE A NOTE FROM YOUR DOCTOR?
I GAVE IT TO THE MAN AT THE DESK.
OH.
BENHAM READ THE NOTE, LOOKED AT SIMON'S PENIS, AND HANDED HIM A SHEET OF BLUE PAPER FROM THE FILE.
TAKE A SEAT IN THE CORRIDOR.
A NURSE WILL COLLECT YOU.

THEY'RE VERY FRAGILE.

I'M SORRY?

VERY FRAGILE. VENEREAL DISEASES. THINK ABOUT IT.

YOU CAN CATCH A COLD OR FLU SIMPLY BY BEING IN THE SAME ROOM AS SOMEONE WHO'S GOT IT.

VENEREAL DISEASES NEED WARMTH AND MOISTURE, AND INTIMATE CONTACT.

NOT MINE, THOUGHT SIMON, BUT HE DIDN'T SAY ANYTHING.

YOU KNOW WHAT I'M DREADING?

TELLING MY WIFE.

TAKE OFF YOUR JACKET AND ROLL UP YOUR RIGHT SLEEVE.

MY JACKET?

FOR THE BLOOD TEST.

OH.

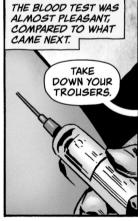

THE BLOOD TEST WAS ALMOST PLEASANT, COMPARED TO WHAT CAME NEXT.

TAKE DOWN YOUR TROUSERS.

HIS PENIS HAD SHRUNK, TIGHTLY PULLED IN ON ITSELF. IT LOOKED GRAY AND WRINKLED.

HE FOUND HIMSELF WANTING TO TELL HER THAT IT WAS NORMALLY MUCH LARGER--

--BUT THEN SHE PICKED UP A METAL INSTRUMENT WITH A WIRE LOOP AT THE END, AND HE WISHED IT WERE EVEN SMALLER.

SQUEEZE YOUR PENIS AT THE BASE AND PUSH FORWARD A FEW TIMES.

SHE STUCK THE LOOP INTO THE HEAD OF HIS PENIS AND TWISTED IT AROUND INSIDE.

HE WINCED IN PAIN.

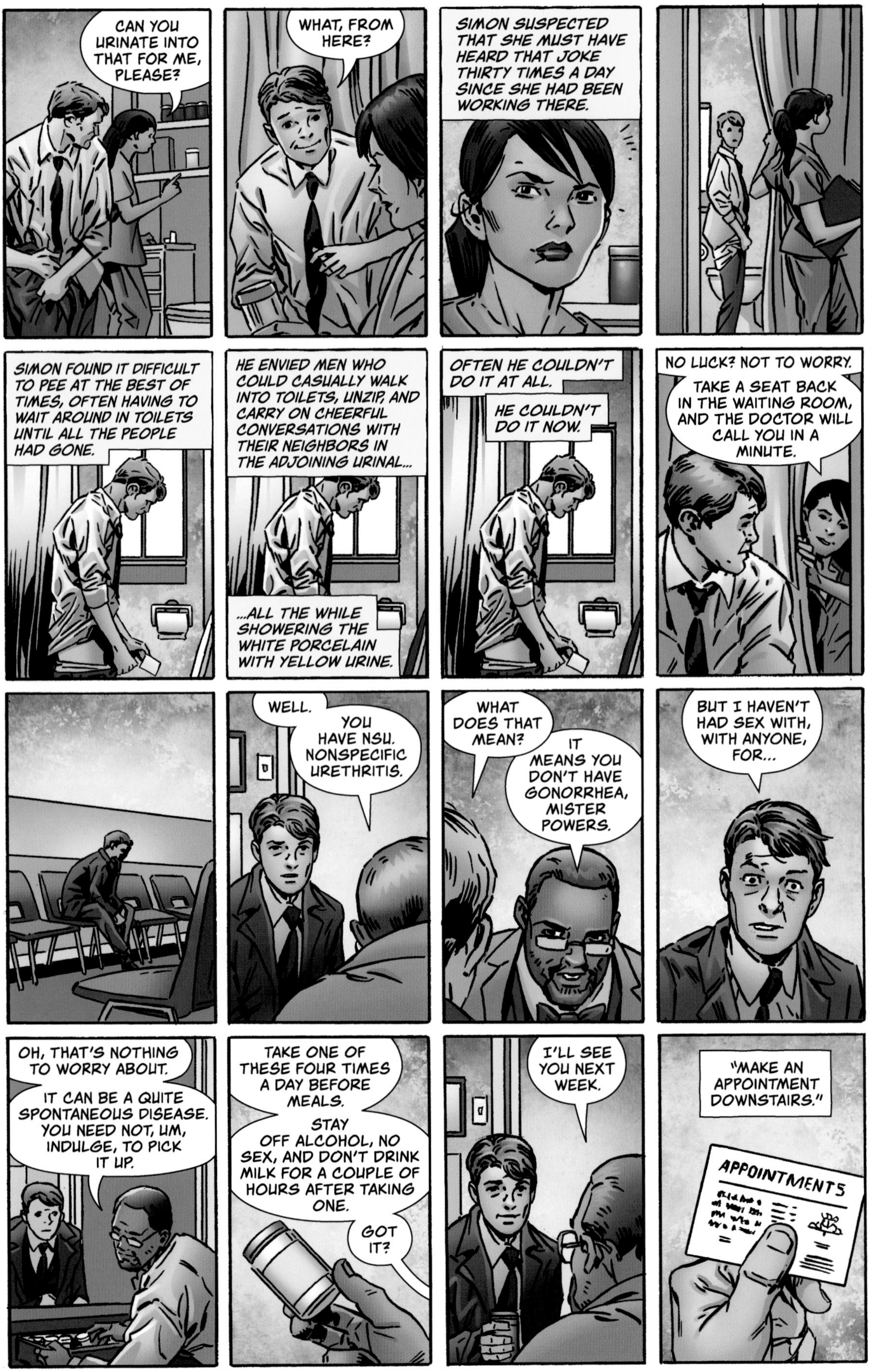
CAN YOU URINATE INTO THAT FOR ME, PLEASE?
WHAT, FROM HERE?
SIMON SUSPECTED THAT SHE MUST HAVE HEARD THAT JOKE THIRTY TIMES A DAY SINCE SHE HAD BEEN WORKING THERE.
SIMON FOUND IT DIFFICULT TO PEE AT THE BEST OF TIMES, OFTEN HAVING TO WAIT AROUND IN TOILETS UNTIL ALL THE PEOPLE HAD GONE.
HE ENVIED MEN WHO COULD CASUALLY WALK INTO TOILETS, UNZIP, AND CARRY ON CHEERFUL CONVERSATIONS WITH THEIR NEIGHBORS IN THE ADJOINING URINAL...
...ALL THE WHILE SHOWERING THE WHITE PORCELAIN WITH YELLOW URINE.
OFTEN HE COULDN'T DO IT AT ALL.
HE COULDN'T DO IT NOW.
NO LUCK? NOT TO WORRY.
TAKE A SEAT BACK IN THE WAITING ROOM, AND THE DOCTOR WILL CALL YOU IN A MINUTE.
WELL.
YOU HAVE NSU. NONSPECIFIC URETHRITIS.
WHAT DOES THAT MEAN?
IT MEANS YOU DON'T HAVE GONORRHEA, MISTER POWERS.
BUT I HAVEN'T HAD SEX WITH, WITH ANYONE, FOR...
OH, THAT'S NOTHING TO WORRY ABOUT.
IT CAN BE A QUITE SPONTANEOUS DISEASE. YOU NEED NOT, UM, INDULGE, TO PICK IT UP.
TAKE ONE OF THESE FOUR TIMES A DAY BEFORE MEALS.
STAY OFF ALCOHOL, NO SEX, AND DON'T DRINK MILK FOR A COUPLE OF HOURS AFTER TAKING ONE.
GOT IT?
I'LL SEE YOU NEXT WEEK.
"MAKE AN APPOINTMENT DOWNSTAIRS."
APPOINTMENTS

SIMON HAD NEVER BEEN ABROAD.

FOREIGN PLACES MADE HIM NERVOUS.

AS THE WEEK WENT ON, THE PAIN WENT AWAY--AND FOUR DAYS LATER SIMON FOUND HIMSELF ABLE TO URINATE WITHOUT FLINCHING.

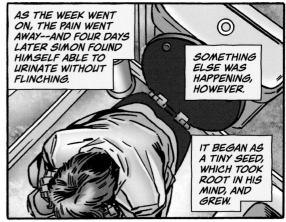

SOMETHING ELSE WAS HAPPENING, HOWEVER.

IT BEGAN AS A TINY SEED, WHICH TOOK ROOT IN HIS MIND, AND GREW.

HE TOLD DR. BENHAM ABOUT IT AT HIS NEXT APPOINTMENT.

YOU'RE SAYING THAT YOU DON'T FEEL YOUR PENIS IS YOUR OWN ANYMORE, THEN, MISTER POWERS?

THAT'S RIGHT, DOCTOR.

I'M AFRAID I DON'T QUITE FOLLOW YOU. IS THERE SOME KIND OF LOSS OF SENSATION?

SIMON COULD FEEL HIS PENIS INSIDE HIS TROUSERS, FELT THE SENSATION OF CLOTH AGAINST FLESH. IN THE DARKNESS IT BEGAN TO STIR.

NOT AT ALL.

I CAN FEEL EVERYTHING LIKE I ALWAYS COULD.

IT'S JUST IT FEELS...WELL, DIFFERENT, I SUPPOSE. LIKE IT ISN'T REALLY PART OF ME ANYMORE. LIKE IT--

--LIKE IT BELONGS TO SOMEONE ELSE.

TO ANSWER YOUR QUESTION, MISTER POWERS, THAT ISN'T A SYMPTOM OF NSU--

--ALTHOUGH IT'S A PERFECTLY VALID PSYCHOLOGICAL REACTION FOR SOME-ONE WHO HAS CONTRACTED IT.

A, UH, FEELING OF DISGUST WITH YOURSELF, PERHAPS, WHICH YOU'VE EXTERNALISED AS A REJECTION OF YOUR GENITALIA.

THAT SOUNDS ABOUT RIGHT, THOUGHT DOCTOR BENHAM. HE HOPED HE HAD GOT THE JARGON CORRECT.

HE HAD NEVER PAID MUCH ATTENTION TO HIS PSYCHOLOGY LECTURES OR TEXTBOOKS, WHICH MIGHT EXPLAIN, OR SO HIS WIFE MAINTAINED, WHY HE WAS CURRENTLY SERVING OUT A STINT IN A LONDON VD CLINIC.

POWERS LOOKED A LITTLE SOOTHED.

I WAS JUST A BIT WORRIED, DOCTOR, THAT'S ALL.

UM, WHAT EXACTLY IS NSU?

COULD BE ANY ONE OF A NUMBER OF THINGS. NSU IS JUST OUR WAY OF SAYING WE DON'T KNOW EXACTLY WHAT IT IS. IT'S NOT GONORRHEA. IT'S NOT CHLAMYDIA. NONSPECIFIC, YOU SEE.

IT'S AN INFECTION, AND IT RESPONDS TO ANTIBIOTICS. WHICH REMINDS ME...
MAKE AN APPOINTMENT DOWNSTAIRS FOR NEXT WEEK.

NO SEX. NO ALCOHOL.

NO SEX? THOUGHT SIMON. NOT BLOODY LIKELY.

BUT WHEN HE WALKED PAST THE PRETTY AUSTRALIAN NURSE IN THE CORRIDOR, HE FELT HIS PENIS BEGIN TO STIR AGAIN, BEGIN TO GET WARM AND TO HARDEN.

BENHAM SAW SIMON THE FOLLOWING WEEK. TESTS SHOWED HE STILL HAD THE DISEASE.

IT'S NOT UNUSUAL FOR IT TO HANG ON FOR THIS LONG. YOU SAY YOU FEEL NO DISCOMFORT?

NO. NONE AT ALL. AND I HAVEN'T SEEN ANY DISCHARGE, EITHER.

YOU'VE STILL GOT IT, I'M AFRAID.

WHAT ABOUT THE OTHER THING, DOCTOR?

WHAT OTHER THING?

I *TOLD* YOU. LAST WEEK. I *TOLD* YOU. THE FEELING THAT MY, UM, MY PENIS WASN'T, ISN'T *MY* PENIS ANYMORE.

OF *COURSE*, THOUGHT BENHAM. IT'S THAT *PATIENT*.

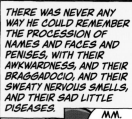

THERE WAS NEVER ANY WAY HE COULD REMEMBER THE PROCESSION OF NAMES AND FACES AND PENISES, WITH THEIR AWKWARDNESS, AND THEIR BRAGGADOCIO, AND THEIR SWEATY NERVOUS SMELLS, AND THEIR SAD LITTLE DISEASES.

MM. WHAT ABOUT IT?

IT'S SPREADING, DOCTOR.

THE WHOLE LOWER HALF OF MY BODY FEELS LIKE IT'S SOMEONE ELSE'S. MY LEGS AND EVERYTHING.

I CAN FEEL THEM, ALL RIGHT, AND THEY GO WHERE I WANT THEM TO GO, BUT SOMETIMES I GET THE FEELING THAT IF THEY WANTED TO GO SOMEWHERE ELSE--IF THEY WANTED TO GO WALKING OFF INTO THE WORLD--THEY COULD, AND THEY'D TAKE ME WITH THEM.

I WOULDN'T BE ABLE TO DO ANYTHING TO STOP IT.

WE'LL CHANGE YOUR ANTIBIOTICS.

IF THE OTHERS HAVEN'T KNOCKED THIS DISEASE OUT BY NOW, I'M SURE THESE WILL.

THEY'LL PROBABLY GET RID OF THIS OTHER FEELING AS WELL.

IT'S PROBABLY JUST A SIDE EFFECT OF THE ANTIBIOTICS.

PERHAPS YOU SHOULD TRY TO GET OUT MORE.

SAME TIME NEXT WEEK. NO SEX, NO BOOZE, NO MILK AFTER THE PILLS.

BENHAM WATCHED HIM CAREFULLY, BUT COULD SEE NOTHING STRANGE ABOUT THE WAY HE WALKED.

ON SATURDAY NIGHT, DOCTOR JEREMY BENHAM AND HIS WIFE, CELIA, ATTENDED A DINNER PARTY HELD BY A PROFESSIONAL COLLEAGUE.

BENHAM SAT NEXT TO A FOREIGN PSYCHIATRIST.

THE TROUBLE WITH TELLING FOLKS YOU'RE A PSYCHIATRIST IS YOU GET TO WATCH THEM TRYING TO ACT NORMAL FOR THE REST OF THE EVENING.

BENHAM SPENT THE REST OF THE EVENING TRYING TO ACT NORMALLY.

HE DRANK TOO MUCH WINE WITH HIS DINNER.

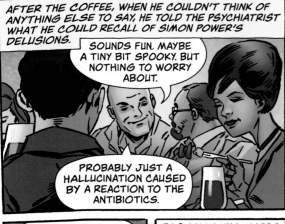

AFTER THE COFFEE, WHEN HE COULDN'T THINK OF ANYTHING ELSE TO SAY, HE TOLD THE PSYCHIATRIST WHAT HE COULD RECALL OF SIMON POWER'S DELUSIONS.

SOUNDS FUN. MAYBE A TINY BIT SPOOKY. BUT NOTHING TO WORRY ABOUT.

PROBABLY JUST A HALLUCINATION CAUSED BY A REACTION TO THE ANTIBIOTICS.

SOUNDS A LITTLE LIKE CAPGRAS'S SYNDROME.

YOU HEARD ABOUT THAT OVER HERE?

BENHAM NODDED.

THEN THOUGHT. THEN SAID:

NO.

WELL, CAPGRAS'S SYNDROME IS THIS FUNKY DELUSION. WHOLE PIECE ON IT IN THE JOURNAL OF AMERICAN PSYCHIATRY ABOUT FIVE YEARS BACK.

BASICALLY, IT'S WHERE A PERSON BELIEVES THAT THE IMPORTANT PEOPLE IN HIS OR HER LIFE--FAMILY MEMBERS, WORKMATES, PARENTS, LOVED ONES, WHAT-EVER--HAVE BEEN REPLACED BY--GET THIS--

--EXACT DOUBLES.

DOESN'T APPLY TO EVERYONE THEY KNOW. JUST SELECTED PEOPLE. OFTEN JUST ONE PERSON IN THEIR LIFE.

NO ACCOMPANYING DELUSIONS, EITHER. JUST THAT ONE THING. ACUTELY EMOTIONALLY DISTURBED PEOPLE WITH PARANOID TENDENCIES.

I RAN INTO A CASE MYSELF, COUPLE, TWO, THREE YEARS BACK.

DID YOU CURE HIM?

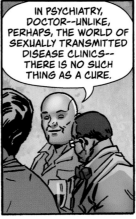

IN PSYCHIATRY, DOCTOR--UNLIKE, PERHAPS, THE WORLD OF SEXUALLY TRANSMITTED DISEASE CLINICS--THERE IS NO SUCH THING AS A CURE.

THERE IS ONLY ADJUSTMENT.

I DON'T SUPPOSE...

I DON'T SUPPOSE THAT ANYONE EVER CHECKED TO SEE IF THOSE PEOPLE HAD BEEN REMOVED AND REPLACED BY EXACT DOUBLES...?

BENHAM, FOR HIS PART, CARRIED ON TRYING TO ACT NORMALLY, WHATEVER THAT WAS, AND FAILED MISERABLY.

HE GOT VERY DRUNK INDEED, STARTED MUTTERING ABOUT "FUCKING COLONIALS"...

...AND HAD A BLAZING ROW WITH HIS WIFE AFTER THE PARTY WAS OVER, NONE OF WHICH WERE PARTICULARLY NORMAL OCCURRENCES.

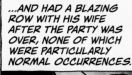

BENHAM'S WIFE LOCKED HIM OUT OF THEIR BEDROOM AFTER THE ARGUMENT.

HE LAY ON THE SOFA DOWNSTAIRS, COVERED BY A CRUMPLED BLANKET, AND MASTURBATED INTO HIS UNDERPANTS, HIS HOT SEED SPURTING ACROSS HIS STOMACH.

IN THE SMALL HOURS HE WAS WOKEN BY A COLD SENSATION AROUND HIS LOINS.

HE WIPED HIMSELF OFF WITH HIS DRESS SHIRT AND RETURNED TO SLEEP.

SIMON WAS UNABLE TO MASTURBATE.

HE WANTED TO, BUT HIS HAND WOULDN'T MOVE. IT LAY BESIDE HIM, HEALTHY, FINE--BUT IT WAS AS IF HE HAD FORGOTTEN HOW TO MAKE IT RESPOND.

WHICH WAS SILLY, WASN'T IT?

WASN'T IT?

HE BEGAN TO SWEAT. IT DRIPPED FROM HIS FACE AND FOREHEAD...

...ONTO THE WHITE COTTON SHEETS, BUT THE REST OF HIS BODY WAS DRY.

CELL BY CELL, SOMETHING WAS REACHING UP INSIDE HIM. IT BRUSHED HIS FACE TENDERLY, LIKE THE KISS OF A LOVER.

IT WAS LICKING HIS THROAT, BREATHING ON HIS CHEEK. TOUCHING HIM.

HE HAD TO GET OUT OF BED.

HE COULDN'T GET OUT OF BED.

HE TRIED TO SCREAM, BUT HIS MOUTH WOULDN'T OPEN. HIS LARYNX REFUSED TO VIBRATE.

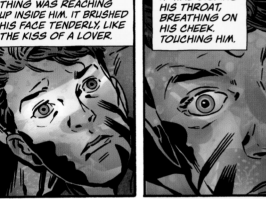

THE CEILING BLURRED: HIS EYES WERE STILL HIS OWN, AND TEARS WERE OOZING OUT OF THEM, DOWN HIS FACE, SOAKING THE PILLOW.

THEY DON'T KNOW WHAT I'VE GOT, HE THOUGHT. THEY SAID I HAD WHAT EVERYONE ELSE GETS. BUT I DIDN'T CATCH THAT. I'VE CAUGHT SOMETHING DIFFERENT.

OR MAYBE...

...IT CAUGHT ME.

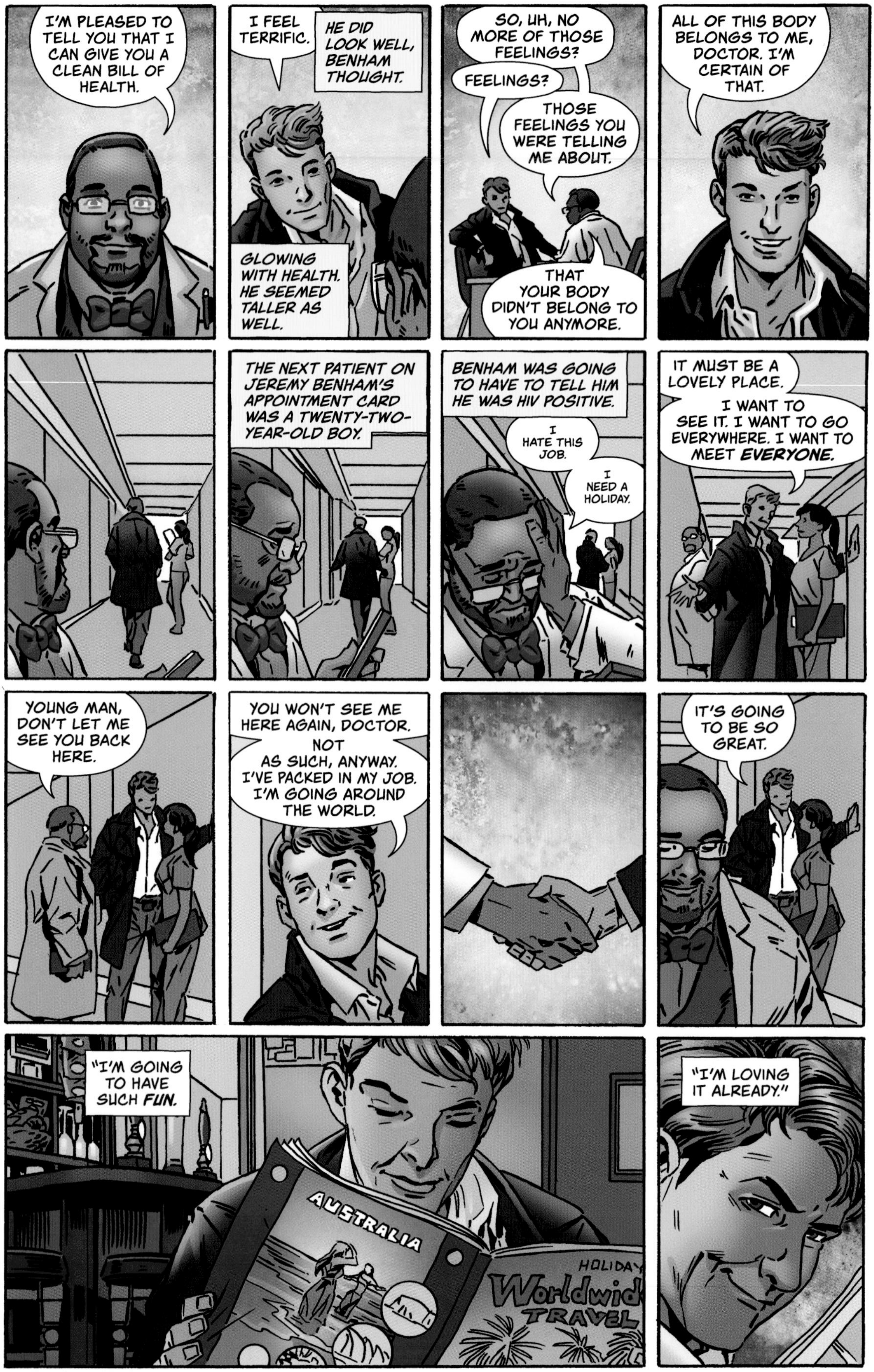
I'M PLEASED TO TELL YOU THAT I CAN GIVE YOU A CLEAN BILL OF HEALTH.
I FEEL TERRIFIC.
HE DID LOOK WELL, BENHAM THOUGHT.
GLOWING WITH HEALTH. HE SEEMED TALLER AS WELL.
SO, UH, NO MORE OF THOSE FEELINGS?
FEELINGS?
THOSE FEELINGS YOU WERE TELLING ME ABOUT.
THAT YOUR BODY DIDN'T BELONG TO YOU ANYMORE.
ALL OF THIS BODY BELONGS TO ME, DOCTOR. I'M CERTAIN OF THAT.
THE NEXT PATIENT ON JEREMY BENHAM'S APPOINTMENT CARD WAS A TWENTY-TWO-YEAR-OLD BOY.
BENHAM WAS GOING TO HAVE TO TELL HIM HE WAS HIV POSITIVE.
I HATE THIS JOB.
I NEED A HOLIDAY.
IT MUST BE A LOVELY PLACE.
I WANT TO SEE IT. I WANT TO GO EVERYWHERE. I WANT TO MEET EVERYONE.
YOUNG MAN, DON'T LET ME SEE YOU BACK HERE.
YOU WON'T SEE ME HERE AGAIN, DOCTOR.
NOT AS SUCH, ANYWAY. I'VE PACKED IN MY JOB. I'M GOING AROUND THE WORLD.
IT'S GOING TO BE SO GREAT.
"I'M GOING TO HAVE SUCH FUN.
AUSTRALIA
HOLIDAY
Worldwid
TRAVEL
"I'M LOVING IT ALREADY."

FEEDERS *and* EATERS

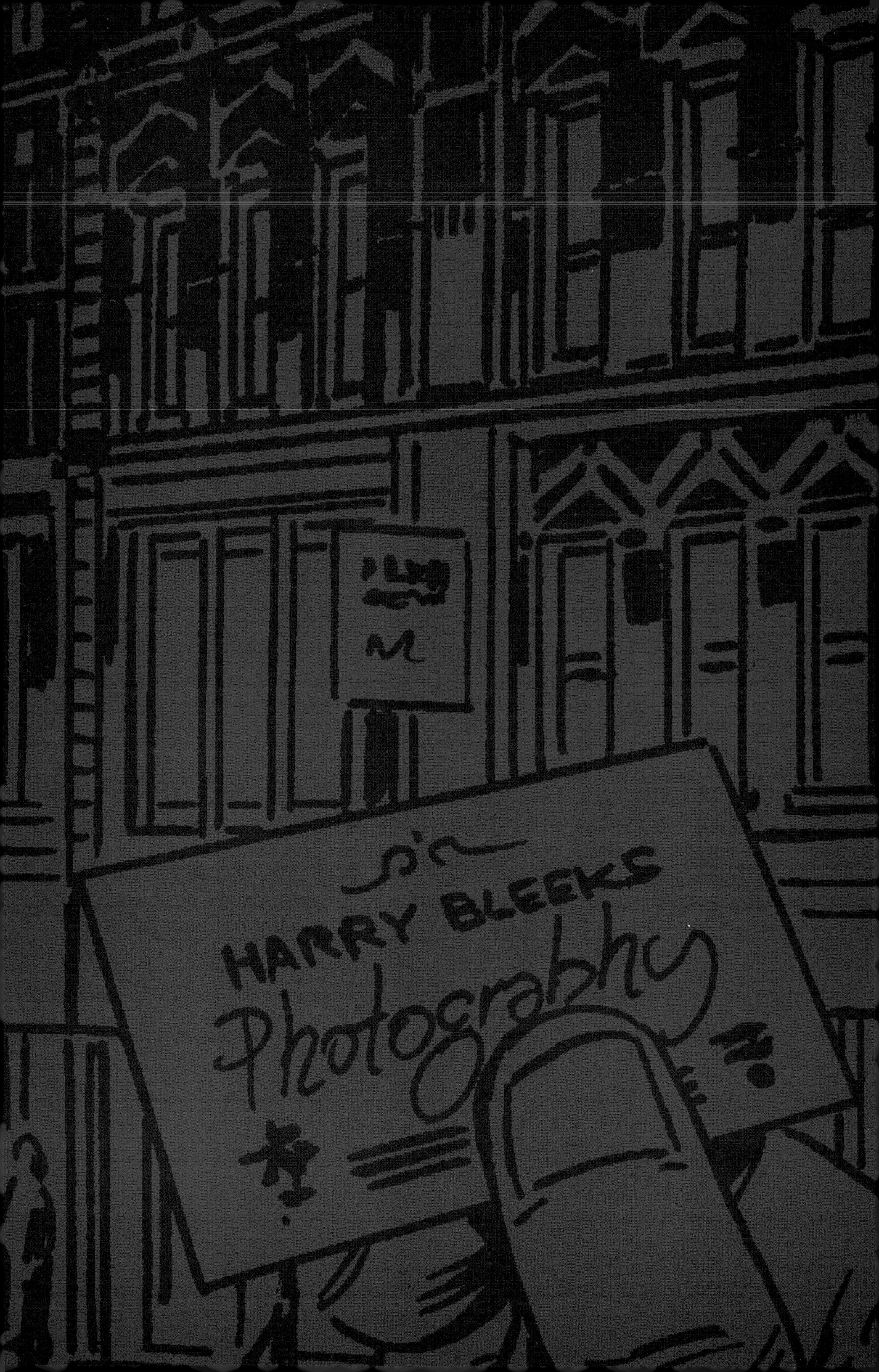
HARRY BLEEKS
Photography

IT WAS LATE ONE NIGHT, AND I WAS COLD.

I'D MISSED MY LAST TRAIN.

SO I WENT TO THE DIOGENES CLUB.

SOMEWHERE WARM TO SIT.

THERE WERE A COUPLE OF OTHER PEOPLE IN THERE, SITTING ALONE AT THEIR TABLES, DERELICTS AND INSOMNIACS HUDDLED OVER THEIR EMPTY PLATES.

DIRTY COATS AND DONKEY JACKETS BUTTONED UP TO THE NECK.

HEY. YOU.

IT WAS A MAN'S VOICE. I KNEW HE WAS TALKING TO ME, NOT TO THE ROOM.

I KNOW YOU. COME HERE. SIT OVER HERE.

I IGNORED IT.

THEN HE SAID MY NAME, AND I TURNED AND LOOKED AT HIM. WHEN SOMEONE KNOWS YOUR NAME, YOU DON'T HAVE ANY OPTION.

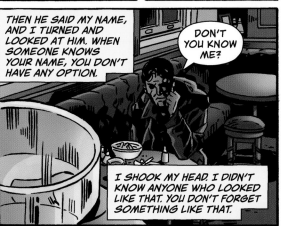

DON'T YOU KNOW ME?

I SHOOK MY HEAD. I DIDN'T KNOW ANYONE WHO LOOKED LIKE THAT. YOU DON'T FORGET SOMETHING LIKE THAT.

IT'S ME.

EDDIE BARROW. COME ON, MATE. YOU KNOW ME.

AND WHEN HE SAID HIS NAME I DID KNOW HIM, MORE OR LESS. I MEAN, I KNEW EDDIE BARROW.

WE HAD WORKED ON A BUILDING SITE TOGETHER, TEN YEARS BACK, DURING MY ONLY REAL FLIRTATION WITH MANUAL WORK.

EDDIE BARROW WAS TALL, AND HEAVILY MUSCLED, WITH A MOVIE STAR SMILE, AND LAZY GOOD LOOKS.

HE WAS EX-POLICE.

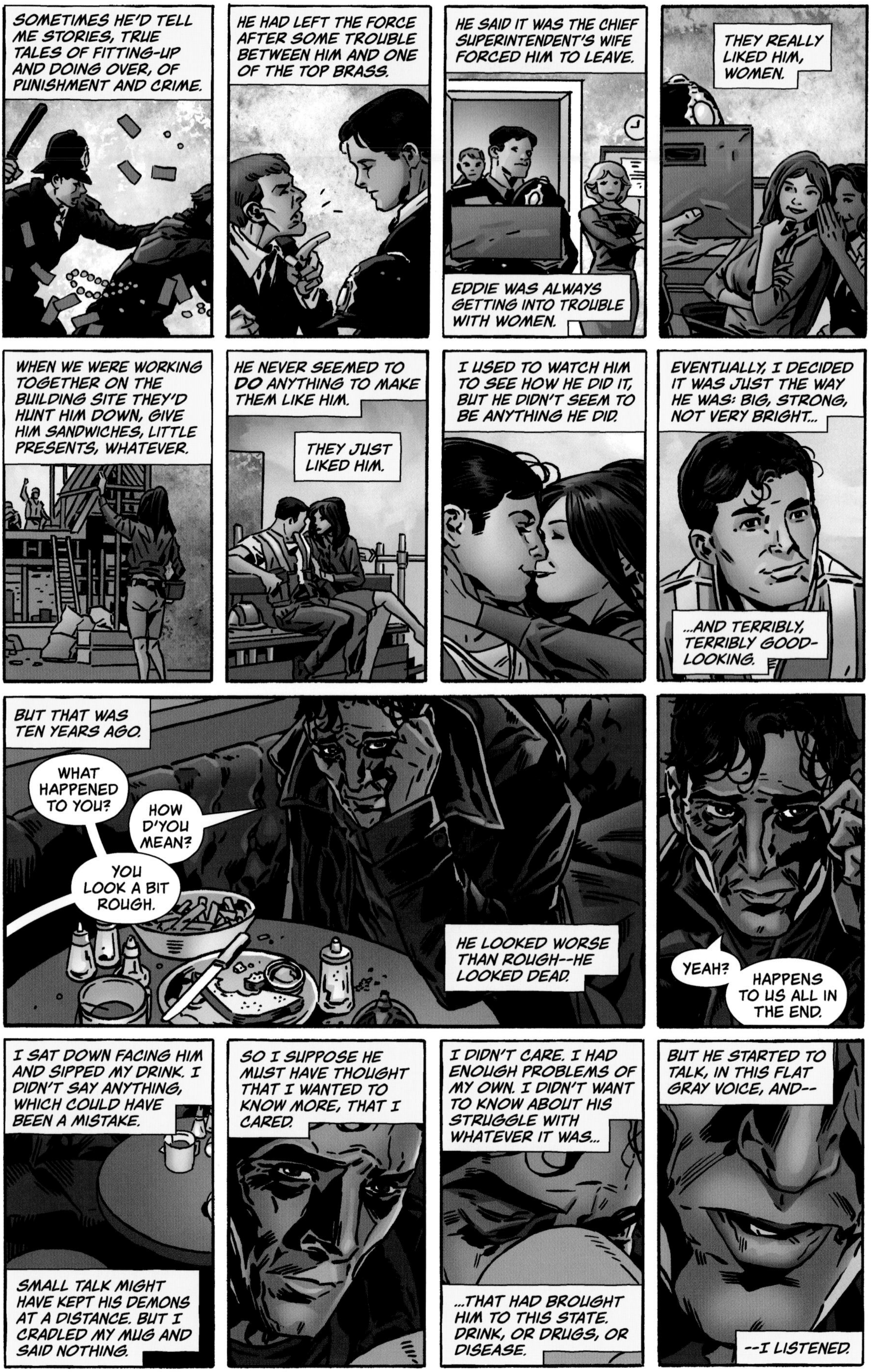

SOMETIMES HE'D TELL ME STORIES, TRUE TALES OF FITTING-UP AND DOING OVER, OF PUNISHMENT AND CRIME.
HE HAD LEFT THE FORCE AFTER SOME TROUBLE BETWEEN HIM AND ONE OF THE TOP BRASS.
HE SAID IT WAS THE CHIEF SUPERINTENDENT'S WIFE FORCED HIM TO LEAVE.
EDDIE WAS ALWAYS GETTING INTO TROUBLE WITH WOMEN.
THEY REALLY LIKED HIM, WOMEN.
WHEN WE WERE WORKING TOGETHER ON THE BUILDING SITE THEY'D HUNT HIM DOWN, GIVE HIM SANDWICHES, LITTLE PRESENTS, WHATEVER.
HE NEVER SEEMED TO DO ANYTHING TO MAKE THEM LIKE HIM.
THEY JUST LIKED HIM.
I USED TO WATCH HIM TO SEE HOW HE DID IT, BUT HE DIDN'T SEEM TO BE ANYTHING HE DID.
EVENTUALLY, I DECIDED IT WAS JUST THE WAY HE WAS: BIG, STRONG, NOT VERY BRIGHT...
...AND TERRIBLY, TERRIBLY GOOD-LOOKING.
BUT THAT WAS TEN YEARS AGO.
WHAT HAPPENED TO YOU?
HOW D'YOU MEAN?
YOU LOOK A BIT ROUGH.
HE LOOKED WORSE THAN ROUGH--HE LOOKED DEAD.
YEAH?
HAPPENS TO US ALL IN THE END.
I SAT DOWN FACING HIM AND SIPPED MY DRINK. I DIDN'T SAY ANYTHING, WHICH COULD HAVE BEEN A MISTAKE.
SMALL TALK MIGHT HAVE KEPT HIS DEMONS AT A DISTANCE. BUT I CRADLED MY MUG AND SAID NOTHING.
SO I SUPPOSE HE MUST HAVE THOUGHT THAT I WANTED TO KNOW MORE, THAT I CARED.
I DIDN'T CARE. I HAD ENOUGH PROBLEMS OF MY OWN. I DIDN'T WANT TO KNOW ABOUT HIS STRUGGLE WITH WHATEVER IT WAS...
...THAT HAD BROUGHT HIM TO THIS STATE. DRINK, OR DRUGS, OR DISEASE.
BUT HE STARTED TO TALK, IN THIS FLAT GRAY VOICE, AND--
--I LISTENED.

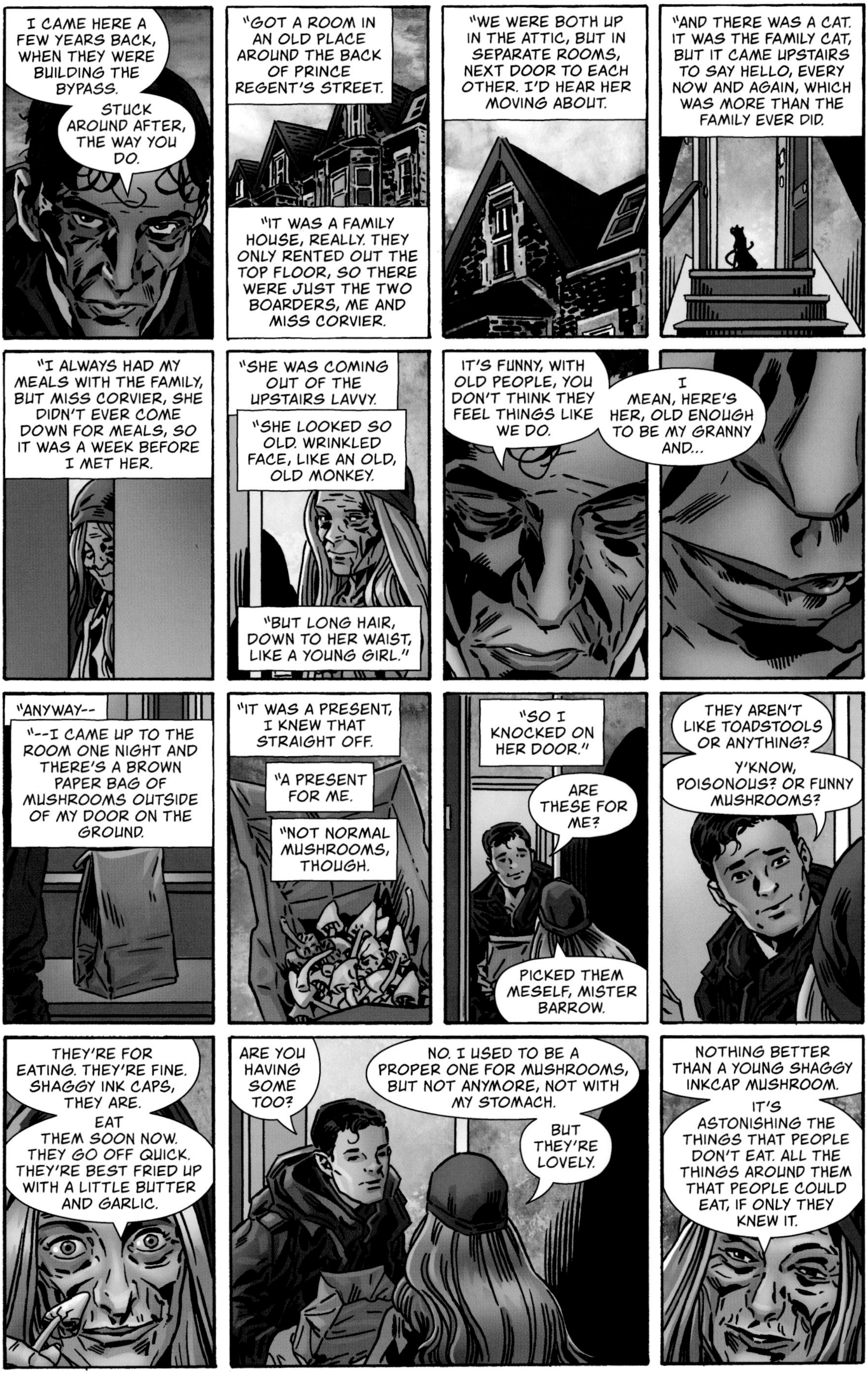
I CAME HERE A FEW YEARS BACK, WHEN THEY WERE BUILDING THE BYPASS.
STUCK AROUND AFTER, THE WAY YOU DO.
"GOT A ROOM IN AN OLD PLACE AROUND THE BACK OF PRINCE REGENT'S STREET.
"IT WAS A FAMILY HOUSE, REALLY. THEY ONLY RENTED OUT THE TOP FLOOR, SO THERE WERE JUST THE TWO BOARDERS, ME AND MISS CORVIER.
"WE WERE BOTH UP IN THE ATTIC, BUT IN SEPARATE ROOMS, NEXT DOOR TO EACH OTHER. I'D HEAR HER MOVING ABOUT.
"AND THERE WAS A CAT. IT WAS THE FAMILY CAT, BUT IT CAME UPSTAIRS TO SAY HELLO, EVERY NOW AND AGAIN, WHICH WAS MORE THAN THE FAMILY EVER DID.
"I ALWAYS HAD MY MEALS WITH THE FAMILY, BUT MISS CORVIER, SHE DIDN'T EVER COME DOWN FOR MEALS, SO IT WAS A WEEK BEFORE I MET HER.
"SHE WAS COMING OUT OF THE UPSTAIRS LAVVY.
"SHE LOOKED SO OLD. WRINKLED FACE, LIKE AN OLD, OLD MONKEY.
"BUT LONG HAIR, DOWN TO HER WAIST, LIKE A YOUNG GIRL."
IT'S FUNNY, WITH OLD PEOPLE, YOU DON'T THINK THEY FEEL THINGS LIKE WE DO.
I MEAN, HERE'S HER, OLD ENOUGH TO BE MY GRANNY AND...
"ANYWAY--
"--I CAME UP TO THE ROOM ONE NIGHT AND THERE'S A BROWN PAPER BAG OF MUSHROOMS OUTSIDE OF MY DOOR ON THE GROUND.
"IT WAS A PRESENT, I KNEW THAT STRAIGHT OFF.
"A PRESENT FOR ME.
"NOT NORMAL MUSHROOMS, THOUGH.
"SO I KNOCKED ON HER DOOR."
ARE THESE FOR ME?
PICKED THEM MESELF, MISTER BARROW.
THEY AREN'T LIKE TOADSTOOLS OR ANYTHING?
Y'KNOW, POISONOUS? OR FUNNY MUSHROOMS?
THEY'RE FOR EATING. THEY'RE FINE. SHAGGY INK CAPS, THEY ARE.
EAT THEM SOON NOW. THEY GO OFF QUICK. THEY'RE BEST FRIED UP WITH A LITTLE BUTTER AND GARLIC.
ARE YOU HAVING SOME TOO?
NO. I USED TO BE A PROPER ONE FOR MUSHROOMS, BUT NOT ANYMORE, NOT WITH MY STOMACH.
BUT THEY'RE LOVELY.
NOTHING BETTER THAN A YOUNG SHAGGY INKCAP MUSHROOM.
IT'S ASTONISHING THE THINGS THAT PEOPLE DON'T EAT. ALL THE THINGS AROUND THEM THAT PEOPLE COULD EAT, IF ONLY THEY KNEW IT.

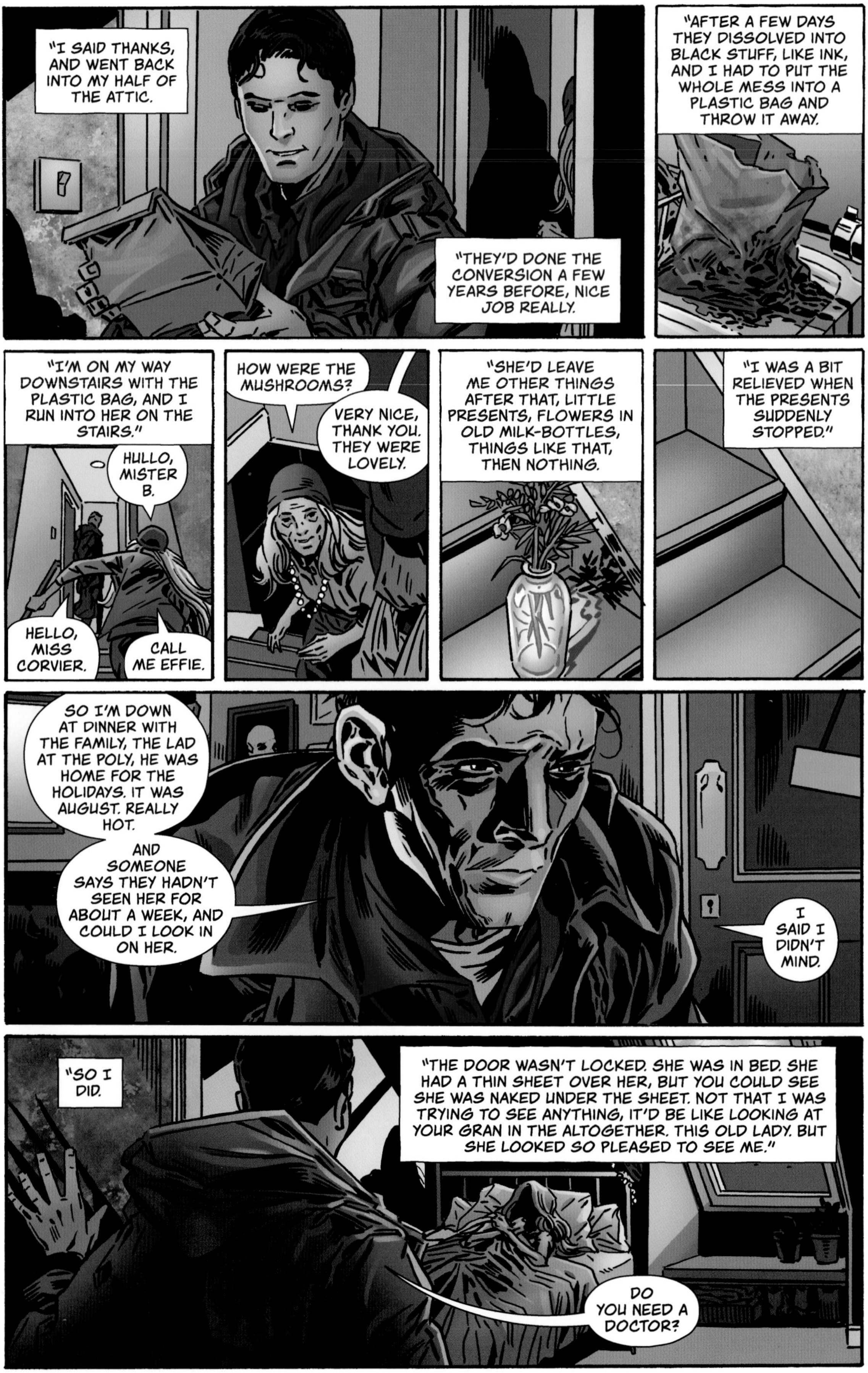
"I SAID THANKS, AND WENT BACK INTO MY HALF OF THE ATTIC.
"THEY'D DONE THE CONVERSION A FEW YEARS BEFORE, NICE JOB REALLY.
"AFTER A FEW DAYS THEY DISSOLVED INTO BLACK STUFF, LIKE INK, AND I HAD TO PUT THE WHOLE MESS INTO A PLASTIC BAG AND THROW IT AWAY.
"I'M ON MY WAY DOWNSTAIRS WITH THE PLASTIC BAG, AND I RUN INTO HER ON THE STAIRS."
HULLO, MISTER B.
HELLO, MISS CORVIER.
CALL ME EFFIE.
HOW WERE THE MUSHROOMS?
VERY NICE, THANK YOU. THEY WERE LOVELY.
"SHE'D LEAVE ME OTHER THINGS AFTER THAT, LITTLE PRESENTS, FLOWERS IN OLD MILK-BOTTLES, THINGS LIKE THAT, THEN NOTHING.
"I WAS A BIT RELIEVED WHEN THE PRESENTS SUDDENLY STOPPED."
SO I'M DOWN AT DINNER WITH THE FAMILY, THE LAD AT THE POLY, HE WAS HOME FOR THE HOLIDAYS. IT WAS AUGUST. REALLY HOT.
AND SOMEONE SAYS THEY HADN'T SEEN HER FOR ABOUT A WEEK, AND COULD I LOOK IN ON HER.
I SAID I DIDN'T MIND.
"SO I DID.
"THE DOOR WASN'T LOCKED. SHE WAS IN BED. SHE HAD A THIN SHEET OVER HER, BUT YOU COULD SEE SHE WAS NAKED UNDER THE SHEET. NOT THAT I WAS TRYING TO SEE ANYTHING, IT'D BE LIKE LOOKING AT YOUR GRAN IN THE ALTOGETHER. THIS OLD LADY. BUT SHE LOOKED SO PLEASED TO SEE ME."
DO YOU NEED A DOCTOR?

I'M NOT ILL, I'M HUNGRY. THAT'S ALL.

ARE YOU SURE?

BECAUSE I CAN CALL SOMEONE, IT'S NOT A BOTHER. THEY'LL COME OUT FOR OLD PEOPLE.

EDWARD? I DON'T WANT TO BE A BURDEN ON ANYONE, BUT I'M SO HUNGRY.

RIGHT. I'LL GET YOU SOMETHING TO EAT. SOMETHING EASY ON YOUR TUMMY.

"THAT'S WHEN SHE SURPRISES ME. SHE LOOKS EMBARRASSED."

MEAT.

IT'S GOT TO BE FRESH MEAT, AND RAW. I WON'T LET ANYONE ELSE COOK FOR ME.

MEAT. PLEASE, EDWARD.

"NOT A PROBLEM I SAYS, AND I GO DOWNSTAIRS.

"I THOUGHT FOR A MOMENT ABOUT NICKING IT FROM THE CAT'S BOWL...

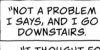

...BUT OF COURSE I DIDN'T.

"IT WAS LIKE, I KNEW SHE WANTED IT, SO I HAD TO DO IT.

"I HAD NO CHOICE.

BEEF MINCE

"I WENT TO SAFEWAYS, AND I BROUGHT HER A PACKET OF BEST GROUND SIRLOIN.

"THE CAT SMELLED IT."

YOU GET DOWN, PUSS. IT'S NOT FOR YOU. IT'S FOR MISS CORVIER AND SHE'S NOT FEELING WELL, AND SHE'S GOING TO NEED IT FOR HER SUPPER.

"THE THING MEWED AT ME AS IF IT HADN'T BEEN FED IN A WEEK, WHICH I KNEW WASN'T TRUE BECAUSE ITS BOWL WAS STILL HALF FULL. STUPID, THAT CAT WAS."

COME IN.

THANK YOU, EDWARD. YOU'VE A GOOD HEART.

"AND SHE STARTS TO TEAR OFF THE PLASTIC WRAP, THERE IN THE BED. THERE'S A PUDDLE OF BROWN BLOOD UNDER THE PLASTIC TRAY, AND IT DRIPS ONTO HER SHEET, BUT SHE DOESN'T NOTICE.

"MAKES ME SHIVER.

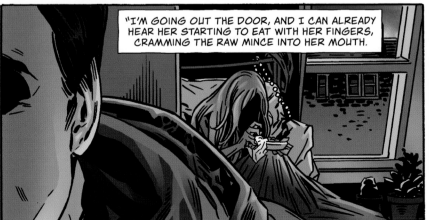

"I'M GOING OUT THE DOOR, AND I CAN ALREADY HEAR HER STARTING TO EAT WITH HER FINGERS, CRAMMING THE RAW MINCE INTO HER MOUTH.

"AND SHE HADN'T GOT OUT OF BED.

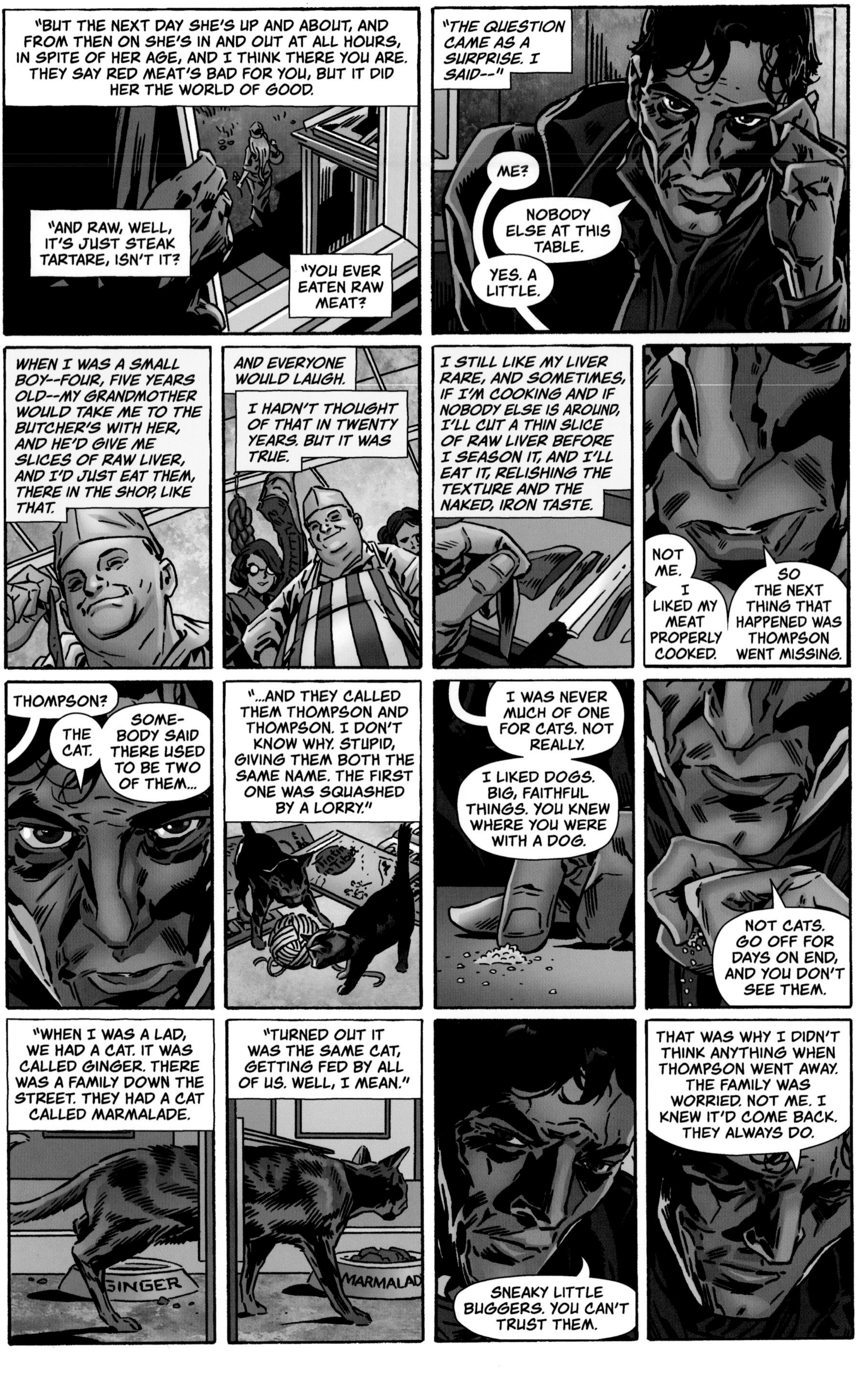
"BUT THE NEXT DAY SHE'S UP AND ABOUT, AND FROM THEN ON SHE'S IN AND OUT AT ALL HOURS, IN SPITE OF HER AGE, AND I THINK THERE YOU ARE. THEY SAY RED MEAT'S BAD FOR YOU, BUT IT DID HER THE WORLD OF GOOD.
"AND RAW, WELL, IT'S JUST STEAK TARTARE, ISN'T IT?
"YOU EVER EATEN RAW MEAT?
"THE QUESTION CAME AS A SURPRISE. I SAID--"
ME?
NOBODY ELSE AT THIS TABLE.
YES. A LITTLE.
WHEN I WAS A SMALL BOY--FOUR, FIVE YEARS OLD--MY GRANDMOTHER WOULD TAKE ME TO THE BUTCHER'S WITH HER, AND HE'D GIVE ME SLICES OF RAW LIVER, AND I'D JUST EAT THEM, THERE IN THE SHOP, LIKE THAT.
AND EVERYONE WOULD LAUGH.
I HADN'T THOUGHT OF THAT IN TWENTY YEARS. BUT IT WAS TRUE.
I STILL LIKE MY LIVER RARE, AND SOMETIMES, IF I'M COOKING AND IF NOBODY ELSE IS AROUND, I'LL CUT A THIN SLICE OF RAW LIVER BEFORE I SEASON IT, AND I'LL EAT IT, RELISHING THE TEXTURE AND THE NAKED, IRON TASTE.
NOT ME. I LIKED MY MEAT PROPERLY COOKED.
SO THE NEXT THING THAT HAPPENED WAS THOMPSON WENT MISSING.
THOMPSON?
THE CAT.
SOMEBODY SAID THERE USED TO BE TWO OF THEM...
"...AND THEY CALLED THEM THOMPSON AND THOMPSON. I DON'T KNOW WHY. STUPID, GIVING THEM BOTH THE SAME NAME. THE FIRST ONE WAS SQUASHED BY A LORRY."
I WAS NEVER MUCH OF ONE FOR CATS. NOT REALLY.
I LIKED DOGS. BIG, FAITHFUL THINGS. YOU KNEW WHERE YOU WERE WITH A DOG.
NOT CATS. GO OFF FOR DAYS ON END, AND YOU DON'T SEE THEM.
"WHEN I WAS A LAD, WE HAD A CAT. IT WAS CALLED GINGER. THERE WAS A FAMILY DOWN THE STREET. THEY HAD A CAT CALLED MARMALADE.
GINGER
"TURNED OUT IT WAS THE SAME CAT, GETTING FED BY ALL OF US. WELL, I MEAN."
MARMALAD
SNEAKY LITTLE BUGGERS. YOU CAN'T TRUST THEM.
THAT WAS WHY I DIDN'T THINK ANYTHING WHEN THOMPSON WENT AWAY. THE FAMILY WAS WORRIED. NOT ME. I KNEW IT'D COME BACK. THEY ALWAYS DO.

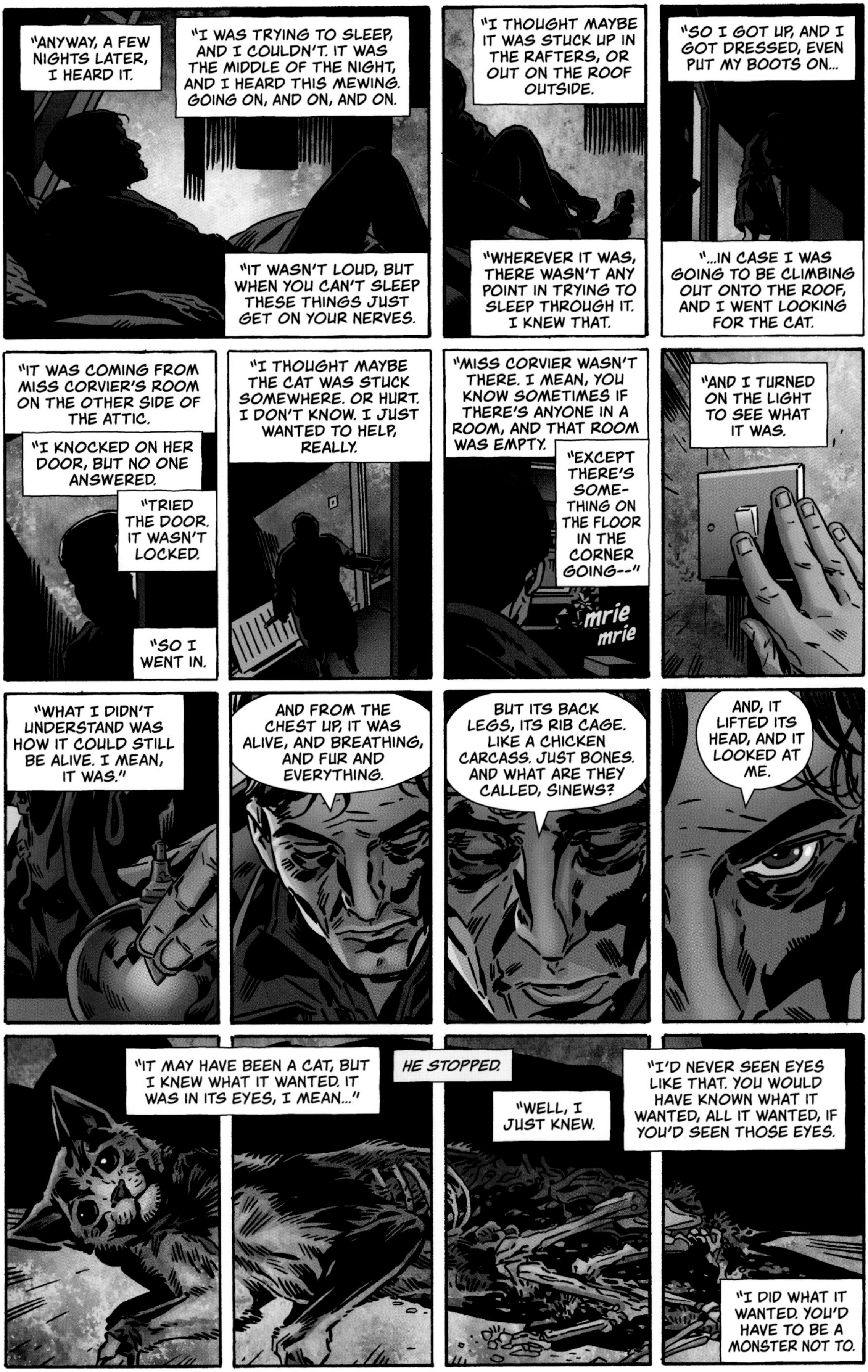
"ANYWAY, A FEW NIGHTS LATER, I HEARD IT.
"I WAS TRYING TO SLEEP, AND I COULDN'T. IT WAS THE MIDDLE OF THE NIGHT, AND I HEARD THIS MEWING. GOING ON, AND ON, AND ON.
"IT WASN'T LOUD, BUT WHEN YOU CAN'T SLEEP THESE THINGS JUST GET ON YOUR NERVES.
"I THOUGHT MAYBE IT WAS STUCK UP IN THE RAFTERS, OR OUT ON THE ROOF OUTSIDE.
"WHEREVER IT WAS, THERE WASN'T ANY POINT IN TRYING TO SLEEP THROUGH IT. I KNEW THAT.
"SO I GOT UP, AND I GOT DRESSED, EVEN PUT MY BOOTS ON...
"...IN CASE I WAS GOING TO BE CLIMBING OUT ONTO THE ROOF, AND I WENT LOOKING FOR THE CAT.
"IT WAS COMING FROM MISS CORVIER'S ROOM ON THE OTHER SIDE OF THE ATTIC.
"I KNOCKED ON HER DOOR, BUT NO ONE ANSWERED.
"TRIED THE DOOR. IT WASN'T LOCKED.
"SO I WENT IN.
"I THOUGHT MAYBE THE CAT WAS STUCK SOMEWHERE. OR HURT. I DON'T KNOW. I JUST WANTED TO HELP, REALLY.
"MISS CORVIER WASN'T THERE. I MEAN, YOU KNOW SOMETIMES IF THERE'S ANYONE IN A ROOM, AND THAT ROOM WAS EMPTY.
"EXCEPT THERE'S SOMETHING ON THE FLOOR IN THE CORNER GOING--"
mrie
mrie
"AND I TURNED ON THE LIGHT TO SEE WHAT IT WAS.
"WHAT I DIDN'T UNDERSTAND WAS HOW IT COULD STILL BE ALIVE. I MEAN, IT WAS."
AND FROM THE CHEST UP, IT WAS ALIVE, AND BREATHING, AND FUR AND EVERYTHING.
BUT ITS BACK LEGS, ITS RIB CAGE. LIKE A CHICKEN CARCASS. JUST BONES. AND WHAT ARE THEY CALLED, SINEWS?
AND, IT LIFTED ITS HEAD, AND IT LOOKED AT ME.
"IT MAY HAVE BEEN A CAT, BUT I KNEW WHAT IT WANTED. IT WAS IN ITS EYES, I MEAN..."
HE STOPPED.
"WELL, I JUST KNEW.
"I'D NEVER SEEN EYES LIKE THAT. YOU WOULD HAVE KNOWN WHAT IT WANTED, ALL IT WANTED, IF YOU'D SEEN THOSE EYES.
"I DID WHAT IT WANTED. YOU'D HAVE TO BE A MONSTER NOT TO.

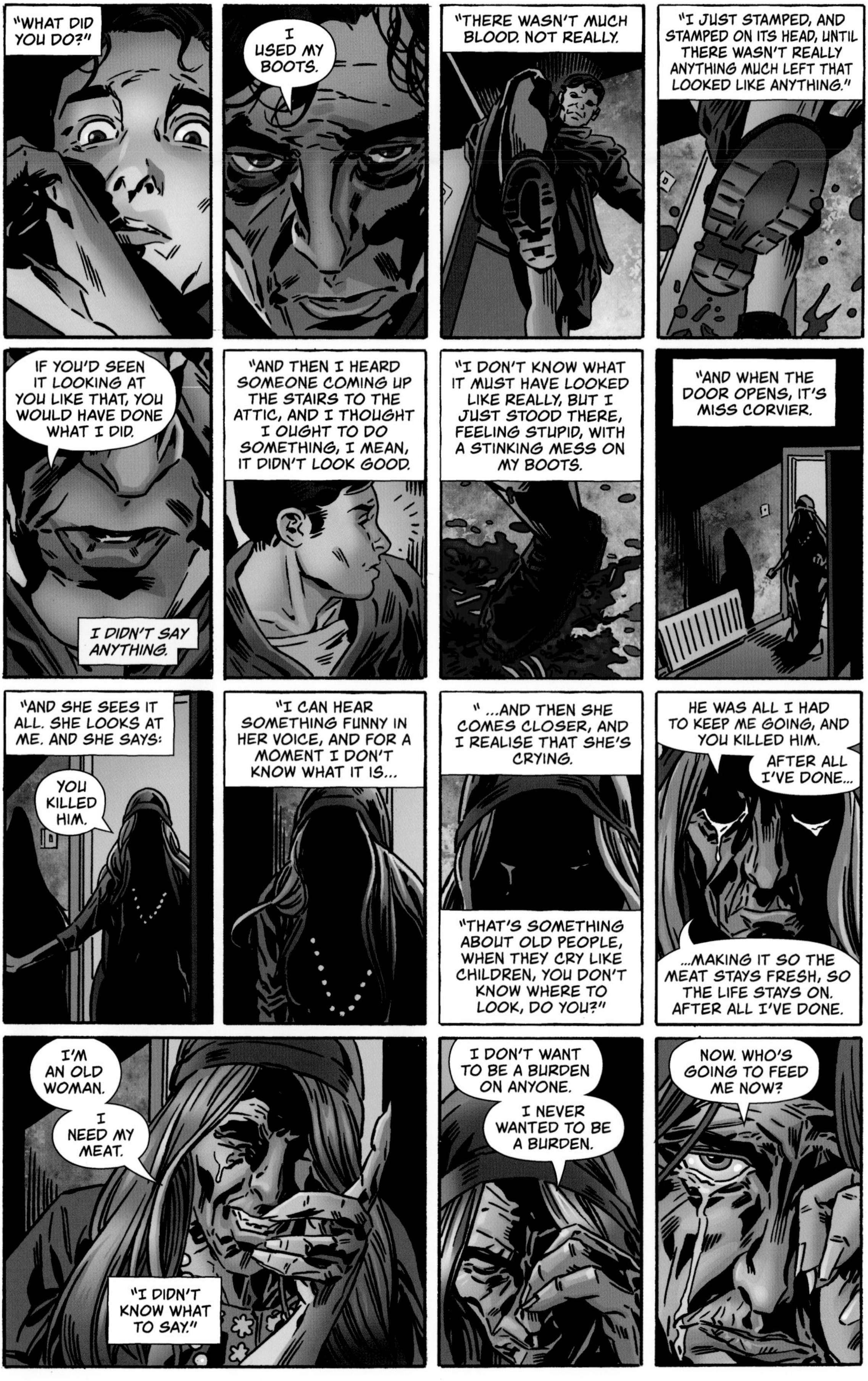
"WHAT DID YOU DO?"
I USED MY BOOTS.
"THERE WASN'T MUCH BLOOD. NOT REALLY.
"I JUST STAMPED, AND STAMPED ON ITS HEAD, UNTIL THERE WASN'T REALLY ANYTHING MUCH LEFT THAT LOOKED LIKE ANYTHING."
IF YOU'D SEEN IT LOOKING AT YOU LIKE THAT, YOU WOULD HAVE DONE WHAT I DID.
I DIDN'T SAY ANYTHING.
"AND THEN I HEARD SOMEONE COMING UP THE STAIRS TO THE ATTIC, AND I THOUGHT I OUGHT TO DO SOMETHING, I MEAN, IT DIDN'T LOOK GOOD.
"I DON'T KNOW WHAT IT MUST HAVE LOOKED LIKE REALLY, BUT I JUST STOOD THERE, FEELING STUPID, WITH A STINKING MESS ON MY BOOTS.
"AND WHEN THE DOOR OPENS, IT'S MISS CORVIER.
"AND SHE SEES IT ALL. SHE LOOKS AT ME. AND SHE SAYS:
YOU KILLED HIM.
"I CAN HEAR SOMETHING FUNNY IN HER VOICE, AND FOR A MOMENT I DON'T KNOW WHAT IT IS...
" ...AND THEN SHE COMES CLOSER, AND I REALISE THAT SHE'S CRYING.
"THAT'S SOMETHING ABOUT OLD PEOPLE, WHEN THEY CRY LIKE CHILDREN, YOU DON'T KNOW WHERE TO LOOK, DO YOU?"
HE WAS ALL I HAD TO KEEP ME GOING, AND YOU KILLED HIM.
AFTER ALL I'VE DONE...
...MAKING IT SO THE MEAT STAYS FRESH, SO THE LIFE STAYS ON. AFTER ALL I'VE DONE.
I'M AN OLD WOMAN.
I NEED MY MEAT.
"I DIDN'T KNOW WHAT TO SAY."
I DON'T WANT TO BE A BURDEN ON ANYONE.
I NEVER WANTED TO BE A BURDEN.
NOW. WHO'S GOING TO FEED ME NOW?

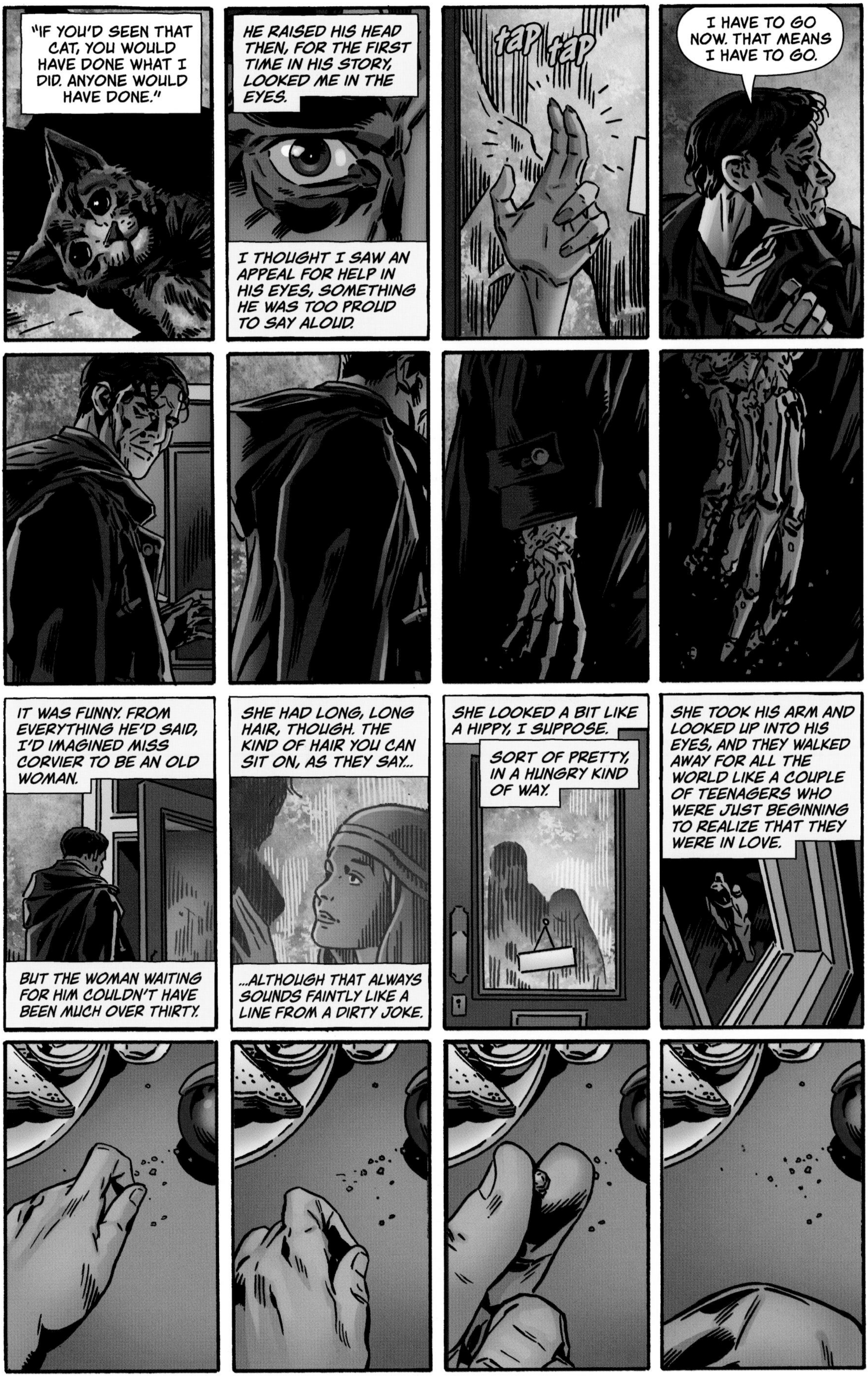
"IF YOU'D SEEN THAT CAT, YOU WOULD HAVE DONE WHAT I DID. ANYONE WOULD HAVE DONE."
HE RAISED HIS HEAD THEN, FOR THE FIRST TIME IN HIS STORY, LOOKED ME IN THE EYES.
I THOUGHT I SAW AN APPEAL FOR HELP IN HIS EYES, SOMETHING HE WAS TOO PROUD TO SAY ALOUD.
tap tap
I HAVE TO GO NOW. THAT MEANS I HAVE TO GO.
IT WAS FUNNY. FROM EVERYTHING HE'D SAID, I'D IMAGINED MISS CORVIER TO BE AN OLD WOMAN.
BUT THE WOMAN WAITING FOR HIM COULDN'T HAVE BEEN MUCH OVER THIRTY.
SHE HAD LONG, LONG HAIR, THOUGH. THE KIND OF HAIR YOU CAN SIT ON, AS THEY SAY...
...ALTHOUGH THAT ALWAYS SOUNDS FAINTLY LIKE A LINE FROM A DIRTY JOKE.
SHE LOOKED A BIT LIKE A HIPPY, I SUPPOSE.
SORT OF PRETTY, IN A HUNGRY KIND OF WAY.
SHE TOOK HIS ARM AND LOOKED UP INTO HIS EYES, AND THEY WALKED AWAY FOR ALL THE WORLD LIKE A COUPLE OF TEENAGERS WHO WERE JUST BEGINNING TO REALIZE THAT THEY WERE IN LOVE.

ON THE MILK TRAIN HOME I SAT OPPOSITE A WOMAN CARRYING A BABY.

IT WAS FLOATING IN FORMALDEHYDE, IN A HEAVY GLASS CONTAINER.

SHE NEEDED TO SELL IT, RATHER URGENTLY, AND ALTHOUGH I WAS EXTREMELY TIRED WE TALKED ABOUT HER REASONS FOR SELLING IT, AND ABOUT OTHER THINGS, FOR THE REST OF THE JOURNEY.

BUT IT IS NOT NECESSARY TO SPEAK FURTHER OF THAT HERE.

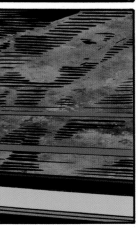

LOOKING
for the GIRL

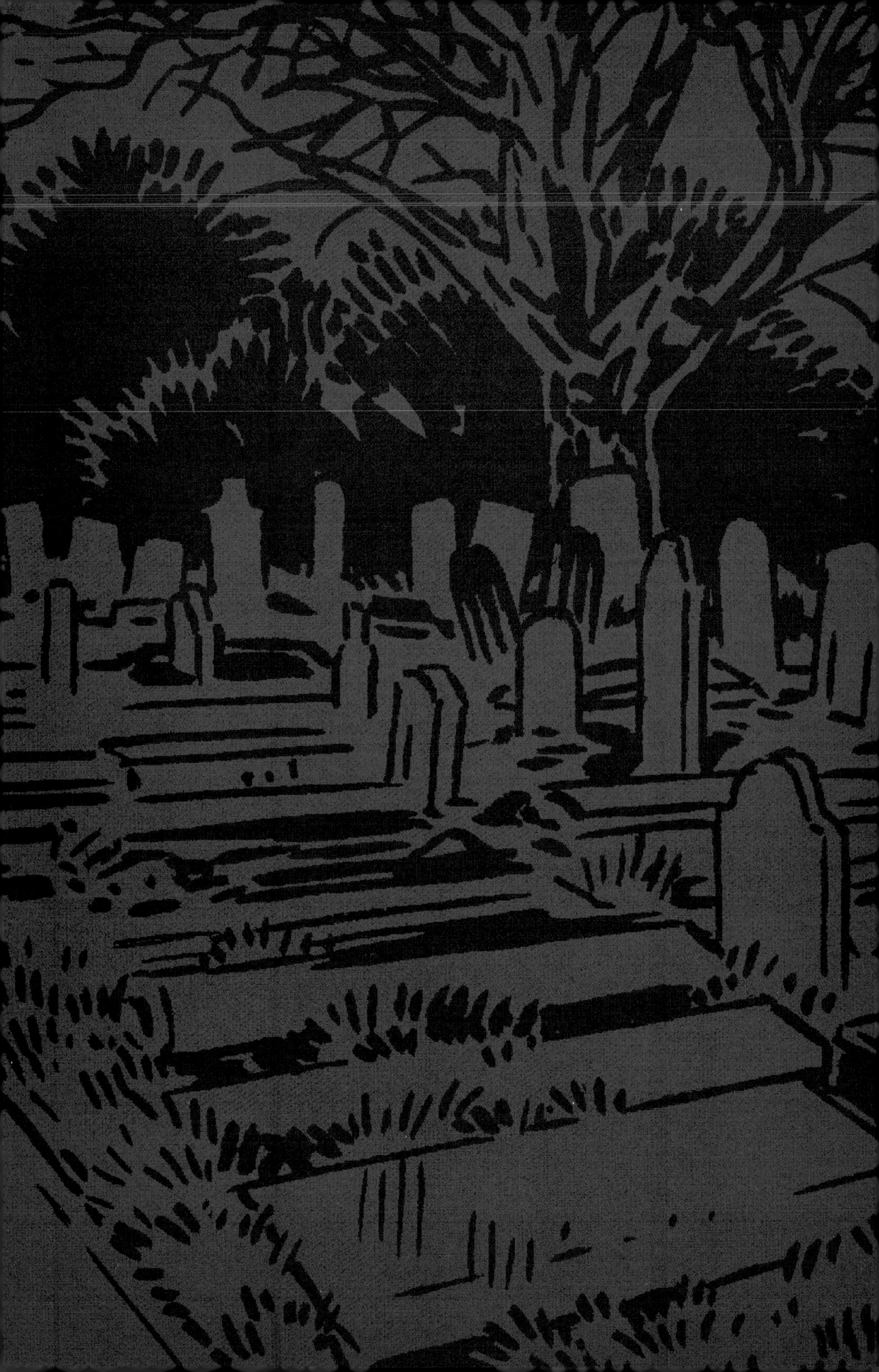

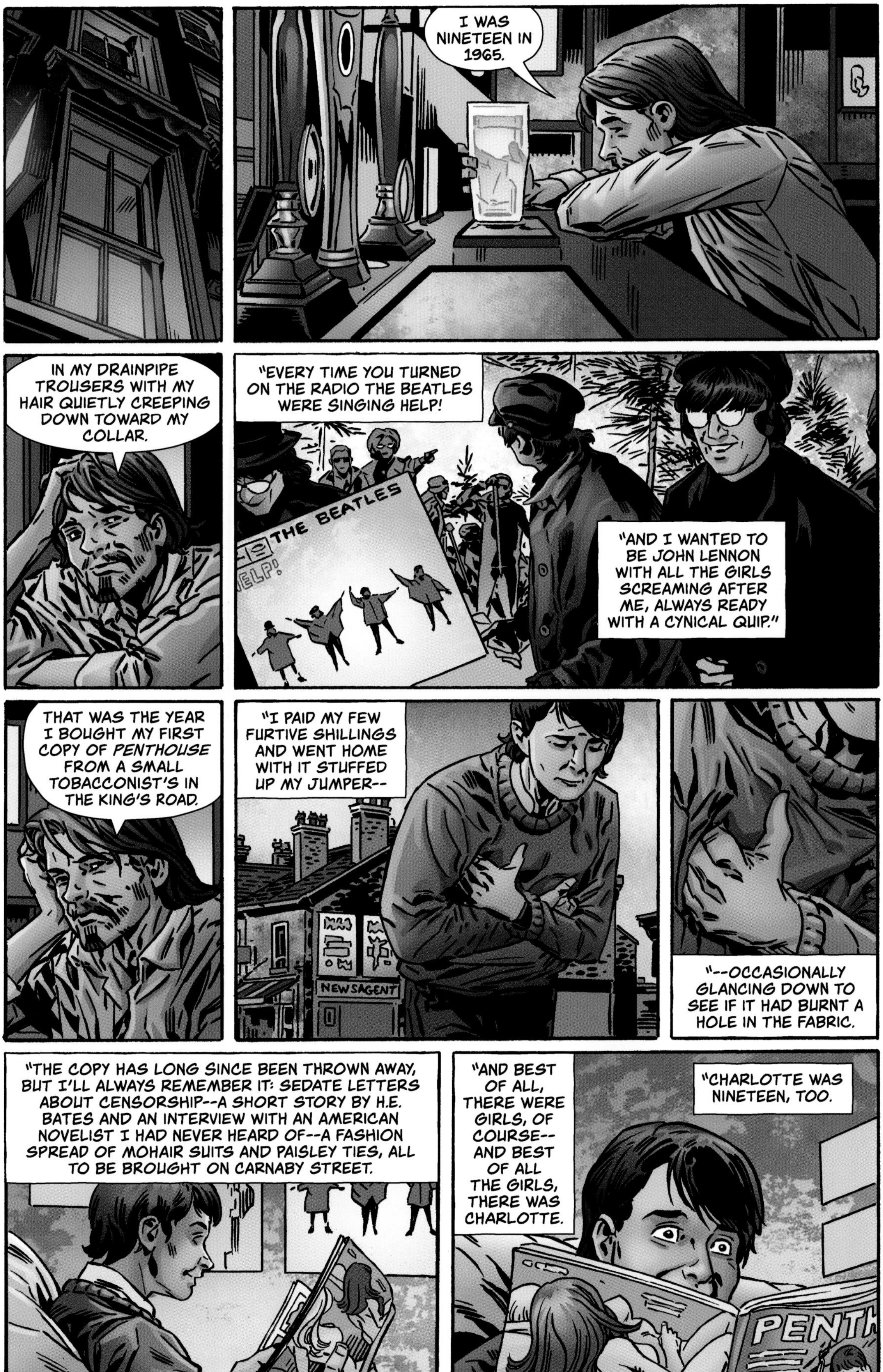
I WAS NINETEEN IN 1965.
IN MY DRAINPIPE TROUSERS WITH MY HAIR QUIETLY CREEPING DOWN TOWARD MY COLLAR.
"EVERY TIME YOU TURNED ON THE RADIO THE BEATLES WERE SINGING HELP!
THE BEATLES
HELP!
"AND I WANTED TO BE JOHN LENNON WITH ALL THE GIRLS SCREAMING AFTER ME, ALWAYS READY WITH A CYNICAL QUIP."
THAT WAS THE YEAR I BOUGHT MY FIRST COPY OF *PENTHOUSE* FROM A SMALL TOBACCONIST'S IN THE KING'S ROAD.
"I PAID MY FEW FURTIVE SHILLINGS AND WENT HOME WITH IT STUFFED UP MY JUMPER--
NEWSAGENT
"--OCCASIONALLY GLANCING DOWN TO SEE IF IT HAD BURNT A HOLE IN THE FABRIC.
"THE COPY HAS LONG SINCE BEEN THROWN AWAY, BUT I'LL ALWAYS REMEMBER IT: SEDATE LETTERS ABOUT CENSORSHIP--A SHORT STORY BY H.E. BATES AND AN INTERVIEW WITH AN AMERICAN NOVELIST I HAD NEVER HEARD OF--A FASHION SPREAD OF MOHAIR SUITS AND PAISLEY TIES, ALL TO BE BROUGHT ON CARNABY STREET.
"AND BEST OF ALL, THERE WERE GIRLS, OF COURSE--AND BEST OF ALL THE GIRLS, THERE WAS CHARLOTTE.
"CHARLOTTE WAS NINETEEN, TOO.
PENTH

"ALL THE GIRLS IN THAT LONG-GONE MAGAZINE SEEMED IDENTICAL WITH THEIR PERFECT PLASTIC FLESH--NOT A HAIR OUT OF PLACE (YOU COULD ALMOST SMELL THE LACQUER)--SMILING WHOLESOMELY AT THE CAMERA WHILE THEIR EYES SQUINTED AT YOU THROUGH FOREST-THICK EYELASHES.

"WHITE LIPSTICK, WHITE TEETH, WHITE BREASTS, BIKINI-BLEACHED.

"I NEVER GAVE A THOUGHT TO THE STRANGE POSITIONS THEY HAD COYLY ARRANGED THEMSELVES INTO TO AVOID SHOWING THE SLIGHTEST CURL OR SHADOW OF PUBIC HAIR.

"I WOULDN'T HAVE KNOWN WHAT I WAS LOOKING AT ANYWAY.

"I HAD EYES ONLY FOR THEIR PALE BOTTOMS AND BREASTS, THEIR CHASTE BUT INVITING COME-ON GLANCES.

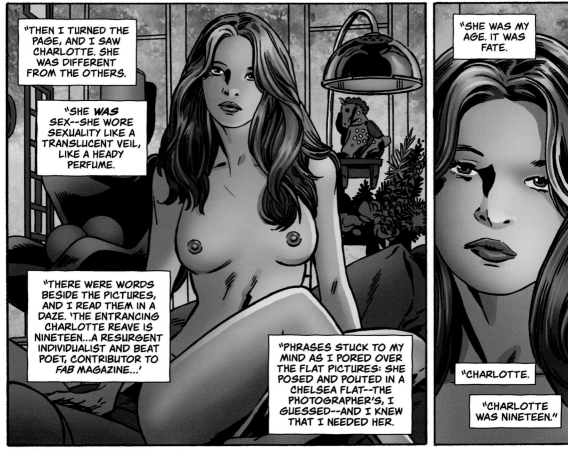

"THEN I TURNED THE PAGE, AND I SAW CHARLOTTE. SHE WAS DIFFERENT FROM THE OTHERS.

"SHE *WAS* SEX--SHE WORE SEXUALITY LIKE A TRANSLUCENT VEIL, LIKE A HEADY PERFUME.

"THERE WERE WORDS BESIDE THE PICTURES, AND I READ THEM IN A DAZE. 'THE ENTRANCING CHARLOTTE REAVE IS NINETEEN...A RESURGENT INDIVIDUALIST AND BEAT POET, CONTRIBUTOR TO FAB MAGAZINE...'

"PHRASES STUCK TO MY MIND AS I PORED OVER THE FLAT PICTURES: SHE POSED AND POUTED IN A CHELSEA FLAT--THE PHOTOGRAPHER'S, I GUESSED--AND I KNEW THAT I NEEDED HER.

"SHE WAS MY AGE. IT WAS FATE.

"CHARLOTTE.

"CHARLOTTE WAS NINETEEN."

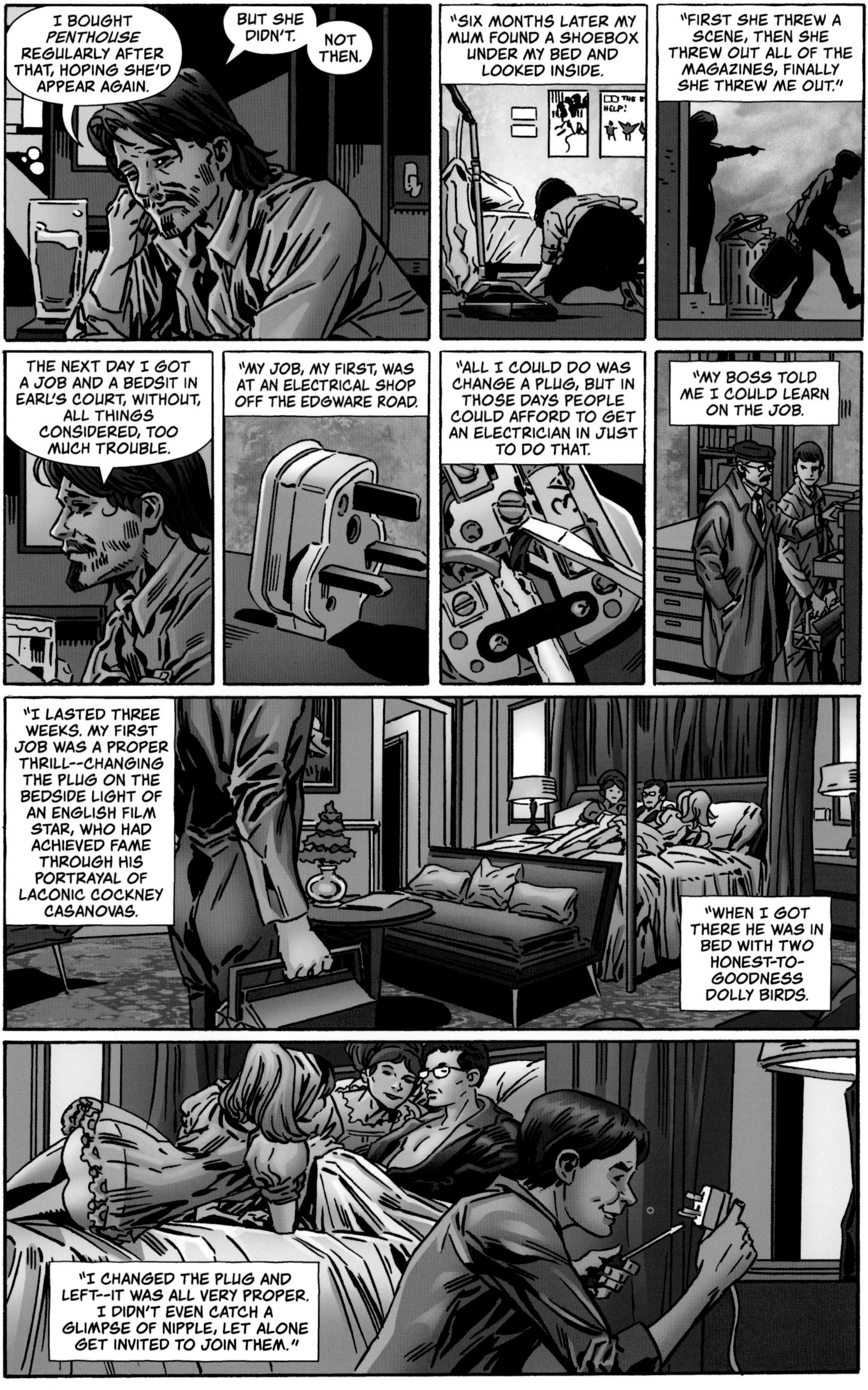
I BOUGHT *PENTHOUSE* REGULARLY AFTER THAT, HOPING SHE'D APPEAR AGAIN.
BUT SHE DIDN'T.
NOT THEN.
"SIX MONTHS LATER MY MUM FOUND A SHOEBOX UNDER MY BED AND LOOKED INSIDE.
"FIRST SHE THREW A SCENE, THEN SHE THREW OUT ALL OF THE MAGAZINES, FINALLY SHE THREW ME OUT."
THE NEXT DAY I GOT A JOB AND A BEDSIT IN EARL'S COURT, WITHOUT, ALL THINGS CONSIDERED, TOO MUCH TROUBLE.
"MY JOB, MY FIRST, WAS AT AN ELECTRICAL SHOP OFF THE EDGWARE ROAD.
"ALL I COULD DO WAS CHANGE A PLUG, BUT IN THOSE DAYS PEOPLE COULD AFFORD TO GET AN ELECTRICIAN IN JUST TO DO THAT.
"MY BOSS TOLD ME I COULD LEARN ON THE JOB.
"I LASTED THREE WEEKS. MY FIRST JOB WAS A PROPER THRILL--CHANGING THE PLUG ON THE BEDSIDE LIGHT OF AN ENGLISH FILM STAR, WHO HAD ACHIEVED FAME THROUGH HIS PORTRAYAL OF LACONIC COCKNEY CASANOVAS.
"WHEN I GOT THERE HE WAS IN BED WITH TWO HONEST-TO-GOODNESS DOLLY BIRDS.
"I CHANGED THE PLUG AND LEFT--IT WAS ALL VERY PROPER. I DIDN'T EVEN CATCH A GLIMPSE OF NIPPLE, LET ALONE GET INVITED TO JOIN THEM."

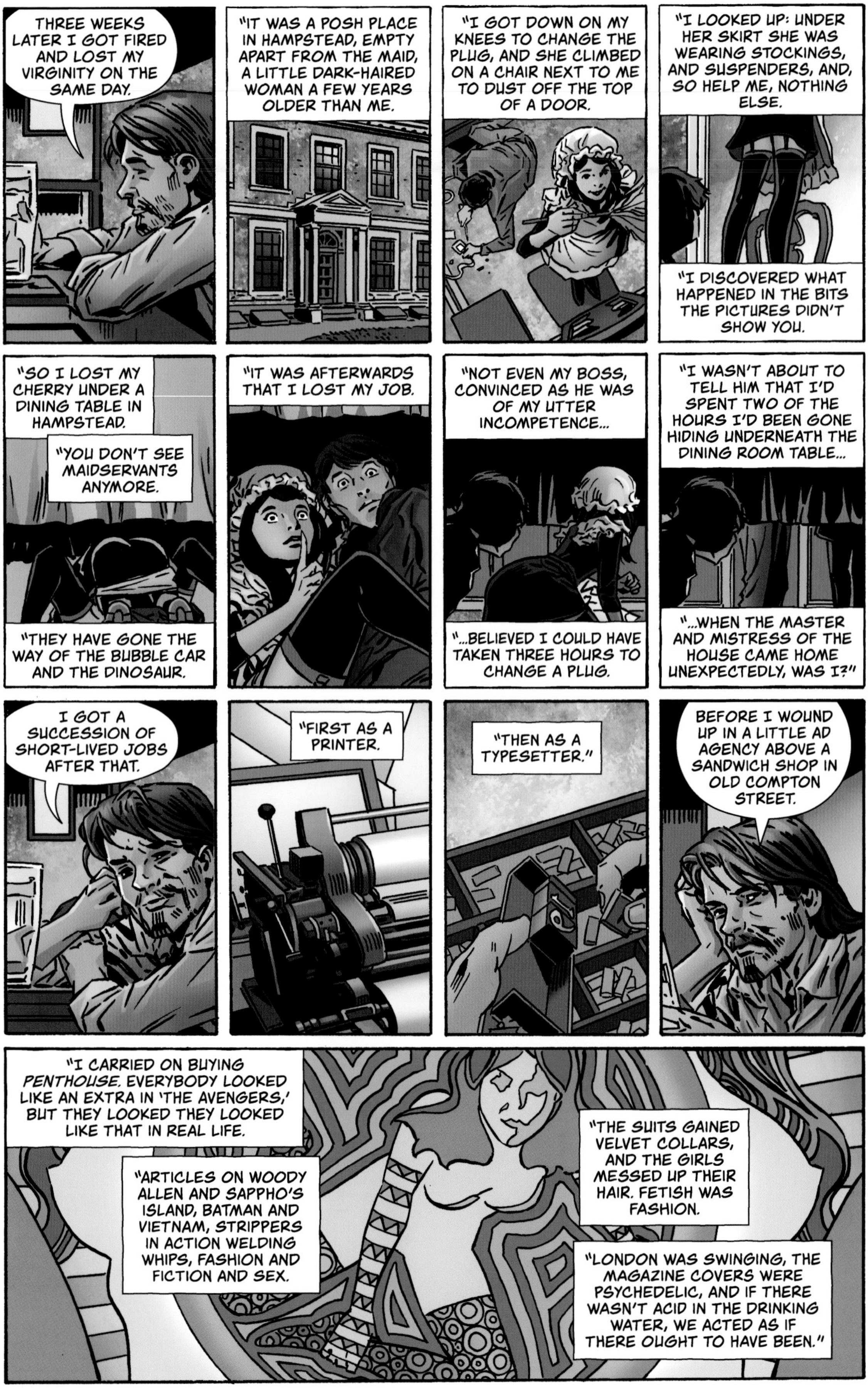
THREE WEEKS LATER I GOT FIRED AND LOST MY VIRGINITY ON THE SAME DAY.
"IT WAS A POSH PLACE IN HAMPSTEAD, EMPTY APART FROM THE MAID, A LITTLE DARK-HAIRED WOMAN A FEW YEARS OLDER THAN ME.
"I GOT DOWN ON MY KNEES TO CHANGE THE PLUG, AND SHE CLIMBED ON A CHAIR NEXT TO ME TO DUST OFF THE TOP OF A DOOR.
"I LOOKED UP: UNDER HER SKIRT SHE WAS WEARING STOCKINGS, AND SUSPENDERS, AND, SO HELP ME, NOTHING ELSE.
"I DISCOVERED WHAT HAPPENED IN THE BITS THE PICTURES DIDN'T SHOW YOU.
"SO I LOST MY CHERRY UNDER A DINING TABLE IN HAMPSTEAD.
"YOU DON'T SEE MAIDSERVANTS ANYMORE.
"THEY HAVE GONE THE WAY OF THE BUBBLE CAR AND THE DINOSAUR.
"IT WAS AFTERWARDS THAT I LOST MY JOB.
"NOT EVEN MY BOSS, CONVINCED AS HE WAS OF MY UTTER INCOMPETENCE...
"...BELIEVED I COULD HAVE TAKEN THREE HOURS TO CHANGE A PLUG.
"I WASN'T ABOUT TO TELL HIM THAT I'D SPENT TWO OF THE HOURS I'D BEEN GONE HIDING UNDERNEATH THE DINING ROOM TABLE...
"...WHEN THE MASTER AND MISTRESS OF THE HOUSE CAME HOME UNEXPECTEDLY, WAS I?"
I GOT A SUCCESSION OF SHORT-LIVED JOBS AFTER THAT.
"FIRST AS A PRINTER.
"THEN AS A TYPESETTER."
BEFORE I WOUND UP IN A LITTLE AD AGENCY ABOVE A SANDWICH SHOP IN OLD COMPTON STREET.
"I CARRIED ON BUYING *PENTHOUSE*. EVERYBODY LOOKED LIKE AN EXTRA IN 'THE AVENGERS,' BUT THEY LOOKED THEY LOOKED LIKE THAT IN REAL LIFE.
"ARTICLES ON WOODY ALLEN AND SAPPHO'S ISLAND, BATMAN AND VIETNAM, STRIPPERS IN ACTION WELDING WHIPS, FASHION AND FICTION AND SEX.
"THE SUITS GAINED VELVET COLLARS, AND THE GIRLS MESSED UP THEIR HAIR. FETISH WAS FASHION.
"LONDON WAS SWINGING, THE MAGAZINE COVERS WERE PSYCHEDELIC, AND IF THERE WASN'T ACID IN THE DRINKING WATER, WE ACTED AS IF THERE OUGHT TO HAVE BEEN."

I SAW CHARLOTTE AGAIN IN 1969, LONG AFTER I'D GIVEN UP ON HER.

I THOUGHT I HAD FORGOTTEN WHAT SHE LOOKED LIKE.

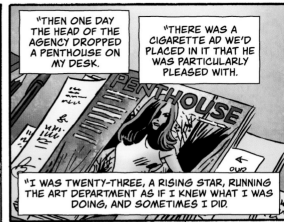

"THEN ONE DAY THE HEAD OF THE AGENCY DROPPED A PENTHOUSE ON MY DESK.

"THERE WAS A CIGARETTE AD WE'D PLACED IN IT THAT HE WAS PARTICULARLY PLEASED WITH.

"I WAS TWENTY-THREE, A RISING STAR, RUNNING THE ART DEPARTMENT AS IF I KNEW WHAT I WAS DOING, AND SOMETIMES I DID.

"I DON'T REMEMBER MUCH ABOUT THE ISSUE ITSELF--ALL I REMEMBER IS CHARLOTTE.

"HAIR WILD AND TAWNY, EYES PROVOCATIVE, SMILING LIKE SHE KNEW ALL THE SECRETS OF LIFE, AND SHE WAS KEEPING THEM CLOSE TO HER NAKED CHEST.

"HER NAME WASN'T CHARLOTTE THEN, IT WAS MELANIE, OR SOMETHING LIKE THAT.

"THE TEXT SAID THAT SHE WAS NINETEEN.

"I WAS LIVING WITH A DANCER CALLED RACHEL AT THE TIME, IN A FLAT IN CAMDEN TOWN.

"SHE WAS THE BEST-LOOKING, MOST DELIGHTFUL WOMAN I'VE EVER KNOWN, WAS RACHEL.

"AND I WENT HOME EARLY WITH THOSE PICTURES OF CHARLOTTE IN MY BRIEFCASE, AND I LOCKED MYSELF IN THE BATHROOM, AND I WANKED MYSELF INTO A DAZE.

"WE BROKE UP SHORTLY AFTER THAT, ME AND RACHEL.

"THE AD AGENCY BOOMED-- EVERYTHING IN THE SIXTIES BOOMED--AND IN 1971 I WAS GIVEN THE TASK OF FINDING 'THE FACE' FOR A CLOTHING LABEL.

"THEY WANTED A GIRL WHO WOULD EPITOMIZE EVERYTHING SEXUAL--WHO WOULD WEAR THEIR CLOTHES AS IF SHE WERE ABOUT TO REACH UP AND RIP THEM OFF--IF SOME MAN DIDN'T GET THERE FIRST.

"AND I KNEW THE PERFECT GIRL: CHARLOTTE.

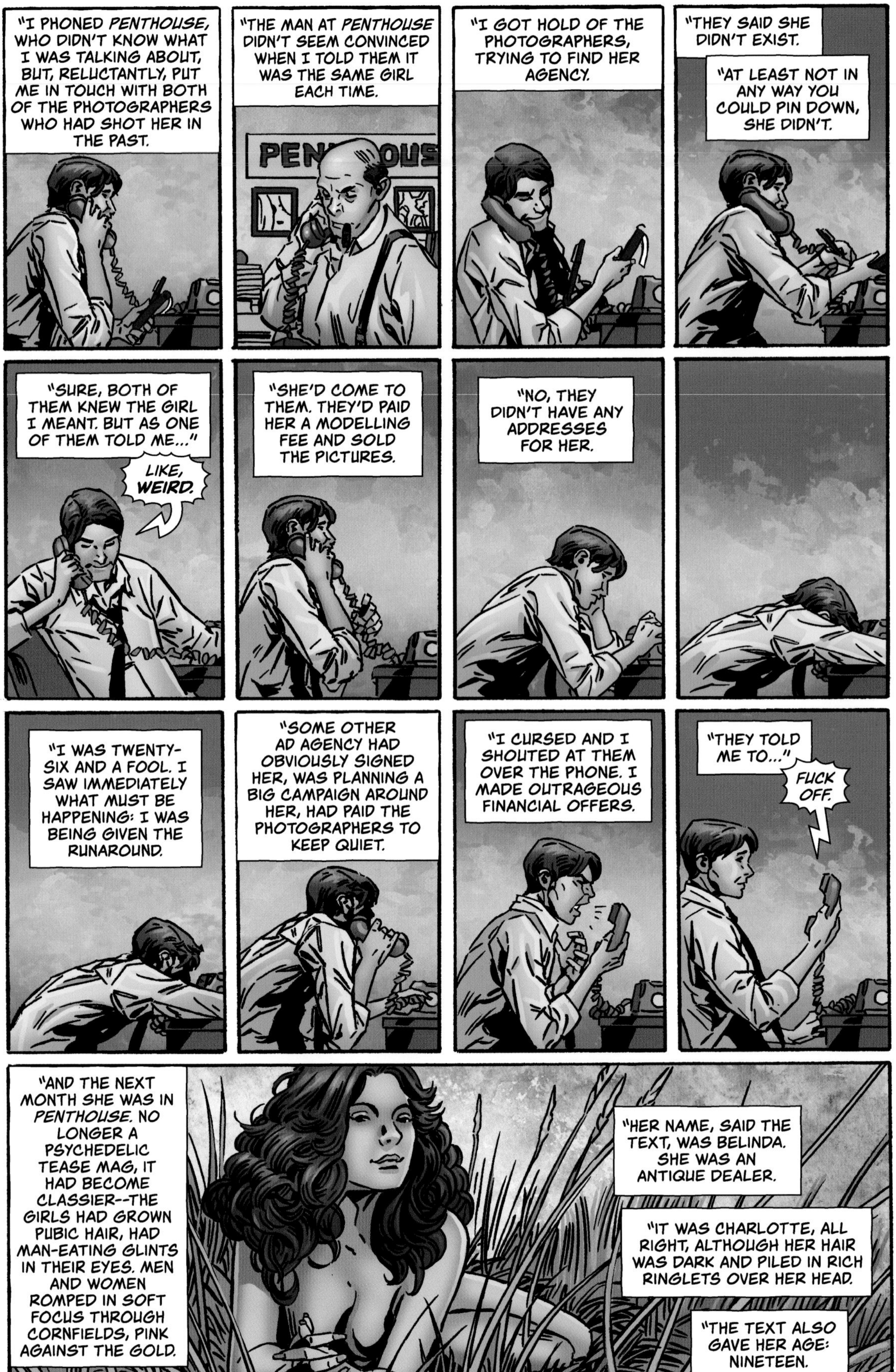
"I PHONED *PENTHOUSE*, WHO DIDN'T KNOW WHAT I WAS TALKING ABOUT, BUT, RELUCTANTLY, PUT ME IN TOUCH WITH BOTH OF THE PHOTOGRAPHERS WHO HAD SHOT HER IN THE PAST.
"THE MAN AT *PENTHOUSE* DIDN'T SEEM CONVINCED WHEN I TOLD THEM IT WAS THE SAME GIRL EACH TIME.
"I GOT HOLD OF THE PHOTOGRAPHERS, TRYING TO FIND HER AGENCY.
"THEY SAID SHE DIDN'T EXIST.
"AT LEAST NOT IN ANY WAY YOU COULD PIN DOWN, SHE DIDN'T.
"SURE, BOTH OF THEM KNEW THE GIRL I MEANT. BUT AS ONE OF THEM TOLD ME..."
LIKE, **WEIRD**.
"SHE'D COME TO THEM. THEY'D PAID HER A MODELLING FEE AND SOLD THE PICTURES.
"NO, THEY DIDN'T HAVE ANY ADDRESSES FOR HER.
"I WAS TWENTY-SIX AND A FOOL. I SAW IMMEDIATELY WHAT MUST BE HAPPENING: I WAS BEING GIVEN THE RUNAROUND.
"SOME OTHER AD AGENCY HAD OBVIOUSLY SIGNED HER, WAS PLANNING A BIG CAMPAIGN AROUND HER, HAD PAID THE PHOTOGRAPHERS TO KEEP QUIET.
"I CURSED AND I SHOUTED AT THEM OVER THE PHONE. I MADE OUTRAGEOUS FINANCIAL OFFERS.
"THEY TOLD ME TO..."
FUCK OFF.
"AND THE NEXT MONTH SHE WAS IN *PENTHOUSE*. NO LONGER A PSYCHEDELIC TEASE MAG, IT HAD BECOME CLASSIER--THE GIRLS HAD GROWN PUBIC HAIR, HAD MAN-EATING GLINTS IN THEIR EYES. MEN AND WOMEN ROMPED IN SOFT FOCUS THROUGH CORNFIELDS, PINK AGAINST THE GOLD.
"HER NAME, SAID THE TEXT, WAS BELINDA. SHE WAS AN ANTIQUE DEALER.
"IT WAS CHARLOTTE, ALL RIGHT, ALTHOUGH HER HAIR WAS DARK AND PILED IN RICH RINGLETS OVER HER HEAD.
"THE TEXT ALSO GAVE HER AGE: NINETEEN.

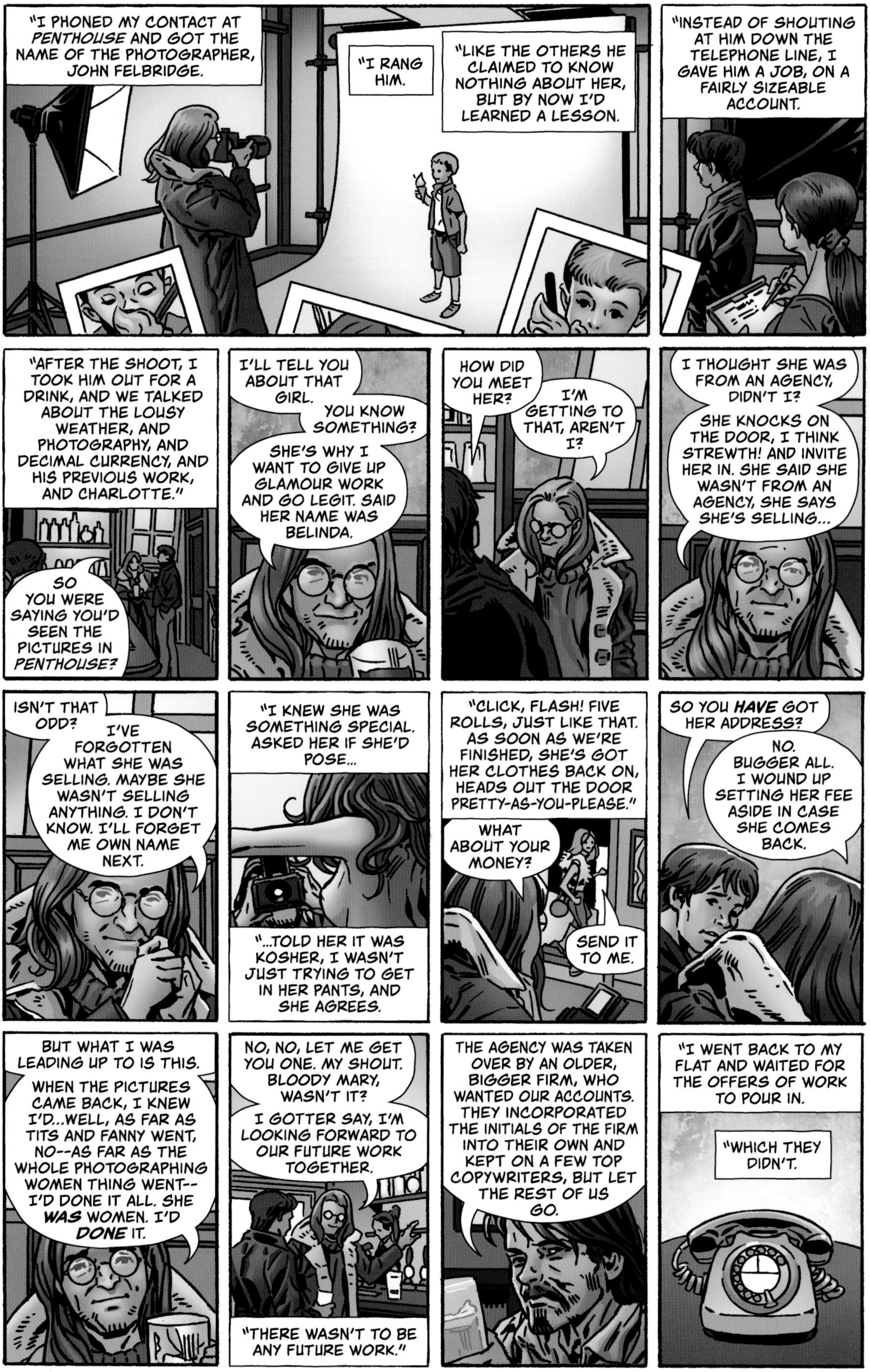
"I PHONED MY CONTACT AT *PENTHOUSE* AND GOT THE NAME OF THE PHOTOGRAPHER, JOHN FELBRIDGE.
"I RANG HIM.
"LIKE THE OTHERS HE CLAIMED TO KNOW NOTHING ABOUT HER, BUT BY NOW I'D LEARNED A LESSON.
"INSTEAD OF SHOUTING AT HIM DOWN THE TELEPHONE LINE, I GAVE HIM A JOB, ON A FAIRLY SIZEABLE ACCOUNT.
"AFTER THE SHOOT, I TOOK HIM OUT FOR A DRINK, AND WE TALKED ABOUT THE LOUSY WEATHER, AND PHOTOGRAPHY, AND DECIMAL CURRENCY, AND HIS PREVIOUS WORK, AND CHARLOTTE."
SO YOU WERE SAYING YOU'D SEEN THE PICTURES IN *PENTHOUSE*?
I'LL TELL YOU ABOUT THAT GIRL.
YOU KNOW SOMETHING?
SHE'S WHY I WANT TO GIVE UP GLAMOUR WORK AND GO LEGIT. SAID HER NAME WAS BELINDA.
HOW DID YOU MEET HER?
I'M GETTING TO THAT, AREN'T I?
I THOUGHT SHE WAS FROM AN AGENCY, DIDN'T I?
SHE KNOCKS ON THE DOOR, I THINK STREWTH! AND INVITE HER IN. SHE SAID SHE WASN'T FROM AN AGENCY, SHE SAYS SHE'S SELLING...
ISN'T THAT ODD?
I'VE FORGOTTEN WHAT SHE WAS SELLING. MAYBE SHE WASN'T SELLING ANYTHING. I DON'T KNOW. I'LL FORGET ME OWN NAME NEXT.
"I KNEW SHE WAS SOMETHING SPECIAL. ASKED HER IF SHE'D POSE...
"...TOLD HER IT WAS KOSHER, I WASN'T JUST TRYING TO GET IN HER PANTS, AND SHE AGREES.
"CLICK, FLASH! FIVE ROLLS, JUST LIKE THAT. AS SOON AS WE'RE FINISHED, SHE'S GOT HER CLOTHES BACK ON, HEADS OUT THE DOOR PRETTY-AS-YOU-PLEASE."
WHAT ABOUT YOUR MONEY?
SEND IT TO ME.
SO YOU **HAVE** GOT HER ADDRESS?
NO. BUGGER ALL. I WOUND UP SETTING HER FEE ASIDE IN CASE SHE COMES BACK.
BUT WHAT I WAS LEADING UP TO IS THIS.
WHEN THE PICTURES CAME BACK, I KNEW I'D...WELL, AS FAR AS TITS AND FANNY WENT, NO--AS FAR AS THE WHOLE PHOTOGRAPHING WOMEN THING WENT--I'D DONE IT ALL. SHE ***WAS*** WOMEN. I'D ***DONE*** IT.
NO, NO, LET ME GET YOU ONE. MY SHOUT. BLOODY MARY, WASN'T IT?
I GOTTER SAY, I'M LOOKING FORWARD TO OUR FUTURE WORK TOGETHER.
"THERE WASN'T TO BE ANY FUTURE WORK."
THE AGENCY WAS TAKEN OVER BY AN OLDER, BIGGER FIRM, WHO WANTED OUR ACCOUNTS. THEY INCORPORATED THE INITIALS OF THE FIRM INTO THEIR OWN AND KEPT ON A FEW TOP COPYWRITERS, BUT LET THE REST OF US GO.
"I WENT BACK TO MY FLAT AND WAITED FOR THE OFFERS OF WORK TO POUR IN.
"WHICH THEY DIDN'T.

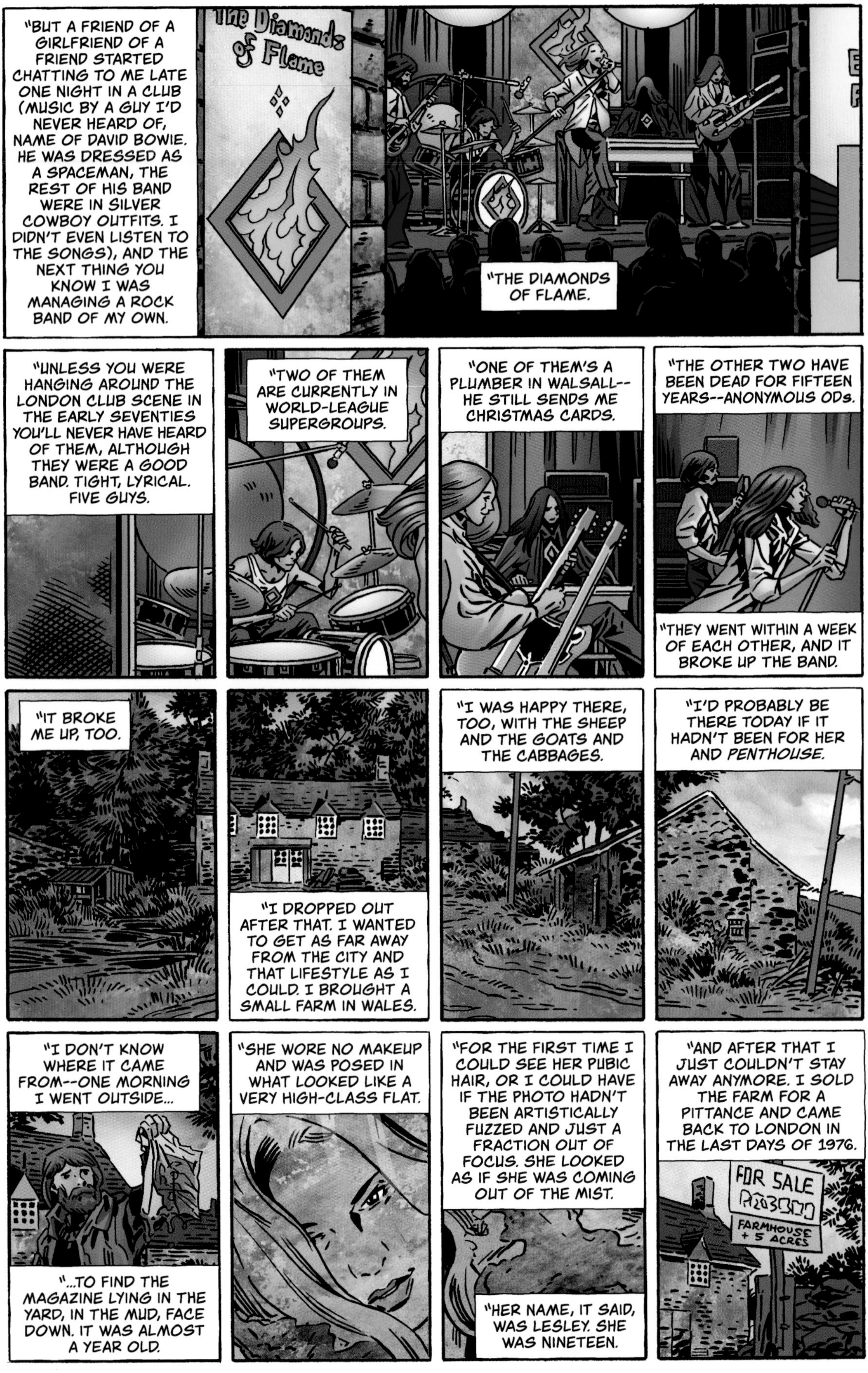
"BUT A FRIEND OF A GIRLFRIEND OF A FRIEND STARTED CHATTING TO ME LATE ONE NIGHT IN A CLUB (MUSIC BY A GUY I'D NEVER HEARD OF, NAME OF DAVID BOWIE. HE WAS DRESSED AS A SPACEMAN, THE REST OF HIS BAND WERE IN SILVER COWBOY OUTFITS. I DIDN'T EVEN LISTEN TO THE SONGS), AND THE NEXT THING YOU KNOW I WAS MANAGING A ROCK BAND OF MY OWN.
The Diamonds of Flame
"THE DIAMONDS OF FLAME.
"UNLESS YOU WERE HANGING AROUND THE LONDON CLUB SCENE IN THE EARLY SEVENTIES YOU'LL NEVER HAVE HEARD OF THEM, ALTHOUGH THEY WERE A GOOD BAND. TIGHT, LYRICAL. FIVE GUYS.
"TWO OF THEM ARE CURRENTLY IN WORLD-LEAGUE SUPERGROUPS.
"ONE OF THEM'S A PLUMBER IN WALSALL--HE STILL SENDS ME CHRISTMAS CARDS.
"THE OTHER TWO HAVE BEEN DEAD FOR FIFTEEN YEARS--ANONYMOUS ODs.
"THEY WENT WITHIN A WEEK OF EACH OTHER, AND IT BROKE UP THE BAND.
"IT BROKE ME UP, TOO.
"I DROPPED OUT AFTER THAT. I WANTED TO GET AS FAR AWAY FROM THE CITY AND THAT LIFESTYLE AS I COULD. I BROUGHT A SMALL FARM IN WALES.
"I WAS HAPPY THERE, TOO, WITH THE SHEEP AND THE GOATS AND THE CABBAGES.
"I'D PROBABLY BE THERE TODAY IF IT HADN'T BEEN FOR HER AND *PENTHOUSE.*
"I DON'T KNOW WHERE IT CAME FROM--ONE MORNING I WENT OUTSIDE...
"...TO FIND THE MAGAZINE LYING IN THE YARD, IN THE MUD, FACE DOWN. IT WAS ALMOST A YEAR OLD.
"SHE WORE NO MAKEUP AND WAS POSED IN WHAT LOOKED LIKE A VERY HIGH-CLASS FLAT.
"FOR THE FIRST TIME I COULD SEE HER PUBIC HAIR, OR I COULD HAVE IF THE PHOTO HADN'T BEEN ARTISTICALLY FUZZED AND JUST A FRACTION OUT OF FOCUS. SHE LOOKED AS IF SHE WAS COMING OUT OF THE MIST.
"HER NAME, IT SAID, WAS LESLEY. SHE WAS NINETEEN.
"AND AFTER THAT I JUST COULDN'T STAY AWAY ANYMORE. I SOLD THE FARM FOR A PITTANCE AND CAME BACK TO LONDON IN THE LAST DAYS OF 1976.
FOR SALE
FARMHOUSE + 5 ACRES

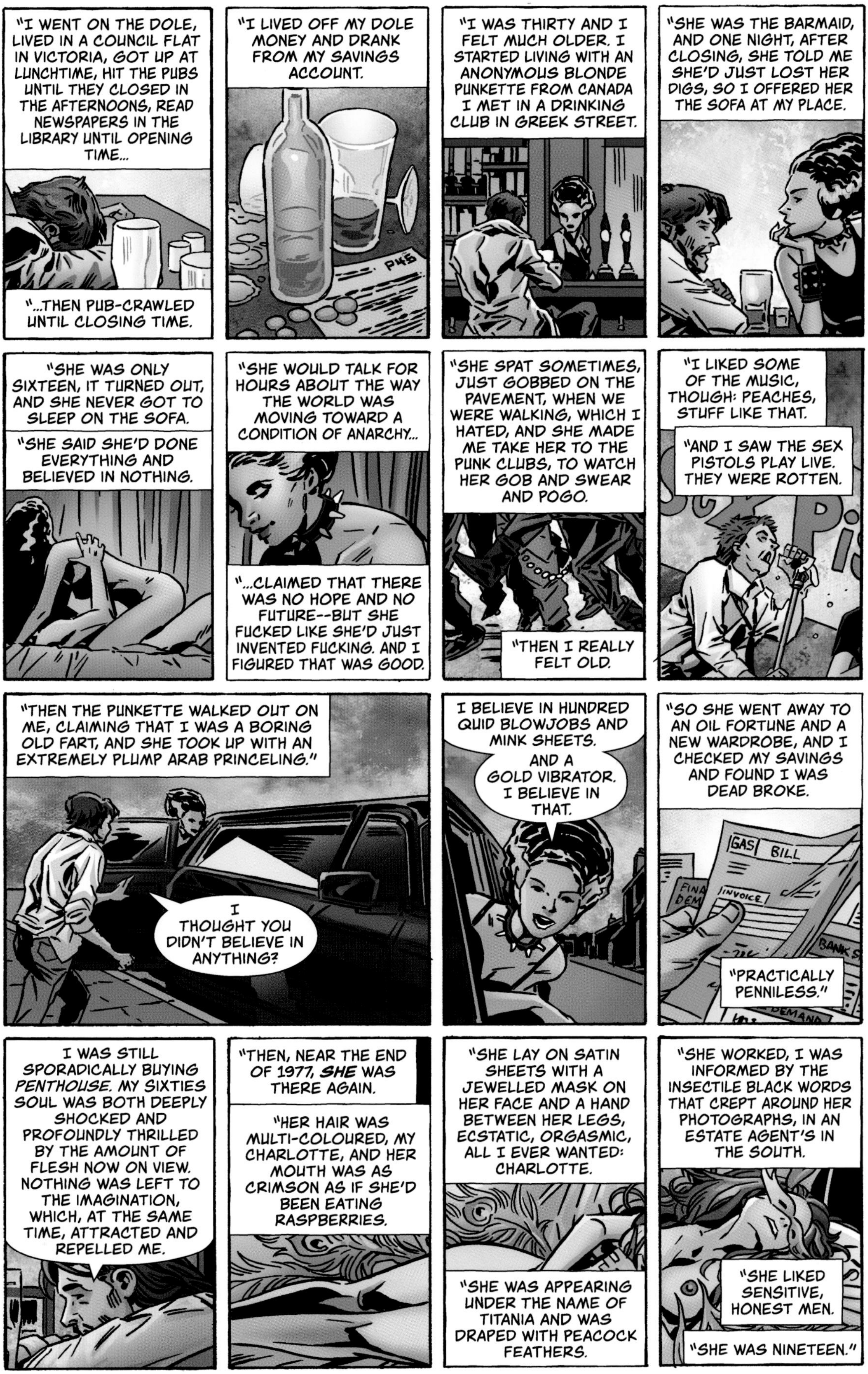
"I WENT ON THE DOLE, LIVED IN A COUNCIL FLAT IN VICTORIA, GOT UP AT LUNCHTIME, HIT THE PUBS UNTIL THEY CLOSED IN THE AFTERNOONS, READ NEWSPAPERS IN THE LIBRARY UNTIL OPENING TIME...
"...THEN PUB-CRAWLED UNTIL CLOSING TIME.
"I LIVED OFF MY DOLE MONEY AND DRANK FROM MY SAVINGS ACCOUNT.
"I WAS THIRTY AND I FELT MUCH OLDER. I STARTED LIVING WITH AN ANONYMOUS BLONDE PUNKETTE FROM CANADA I MET IN A DRINKING CLUB IN GREEK STREET.
"SHE WAS THE BARMAID, AND ONE NIGHT, AFTER CLOSING, SHE TOLD ME SHE'D JUST LOST HER DIGS, SO I OFFERED HER THE SOFA AT MY PLACE.
"SHE WAS ONLY SIXTEEN, IT TURNED OUT, AND SHE NEVER GOT TO SLEEP ON THE SOFA.
"SHE SAID SHE'D DONE EVERYTHING AND BELIEVED IN NOTHING.
"SHE WOULD TALK FOR HOURS ABOUT THE WAY THE WORLD WAS MOVING TOWARD A CONDITION OF ANARCHY...
"...CLAIMED THAT THERE WAS NO HOPE AND NO FUTURE--BUT SHE FUCKED LIKE SHE'D JUST INVENTED FUCKING. AND I FIGURED THAT WAS GOOD.
"SHE SPAT SOMETIMES, JUST GOBBED ON THE PAVEMENT, WHEN WE WERE WALKING, WHICH I HATED, AND SHE MADE ME TAKE HER TO THE PUNK CLUBS, TO WATCH HER GOB AND SWEAR AND POGO.
"THEN I REALLY FELT OLD.
"I LIKED SOME OF THE MUSIC, THOUGH: PEACHES, STUFF LIKE THAT.
"AND I SAW THE SEX PISTOLS PLAY LIVE. THEY WERE ROTTEN.
"THEN THE PUNKETTE WALKED OUT ON ME, CLAIMING THAT I WAS A BORING OLD FART, AND SHE TOOK UP WITH AN EXTREMELY PLUMP ARAB PRINCELING."
I THOUGHT YOU DIDN'T BELIEVE IN ANYTHING?
I BELIEVE IN HUNDRED QUID BLOWJOBS AND MINK SHEETS.
AND A GOLD VIBRATOR. I BELIEVE IN THAT.
"SO SHE WENT AWAY TO AN OIL FORTUNE AND A NEW WARDROBE, AND I CHECKED MY SAVINGS AND FOUND I WAS DEAD BROKE.
GAS BILL
INVOICE
"PRACTICALLY PENNILESS."
I WAS STILL SPORADICALLY BUYING PENTHOUSE. MY SIXTIES SOUL WAS BOTH DEEPLY SHOCKED AND PROFOUNDLY THRILLED BY THE AMOUNT OF FLESH NOW ON VIEW. NOTHING WAS LEFT TO THE IMAGINATION, WHICH, AT THE SAME TIME, ATTRACTED AND REPELLED ME.
"THEN, NEAR THE END OF 1977, SHE WAS THERE AGAIN.
"HER HAIR WAS MULTI-COLOURED, MY CHARLOTTE, AND HER MOUTH WAS AS CRIMSON AS IF SHE'D BEEN EATING RASPBERRIES.
"SHE LAY ON SATIN SHEETS WITH A JEWELLED MASK ON HER FACE AND A HAND BETWEEN HER LEGS, ECSTATIC, ORGASMIC, ALL I EVER WANTED: CHARLOTTE.
"SHE WAS APPEARING UNDER THE NAME OF TITANIA AND WAS DRAPED WITH PEACOCK FEATHERS.
"SHE WORKED, I WAS INFORMED BY THE INSECTILE BLACK WORDS THAT CREPT AROUND HER PHOTOGRAPHS, IN AN ESTATE AGENT'S IN THE SOUTH.
"SHE LIKED SENSITIVE, HONEST MEN.
"SHE WAS NINETEEN."

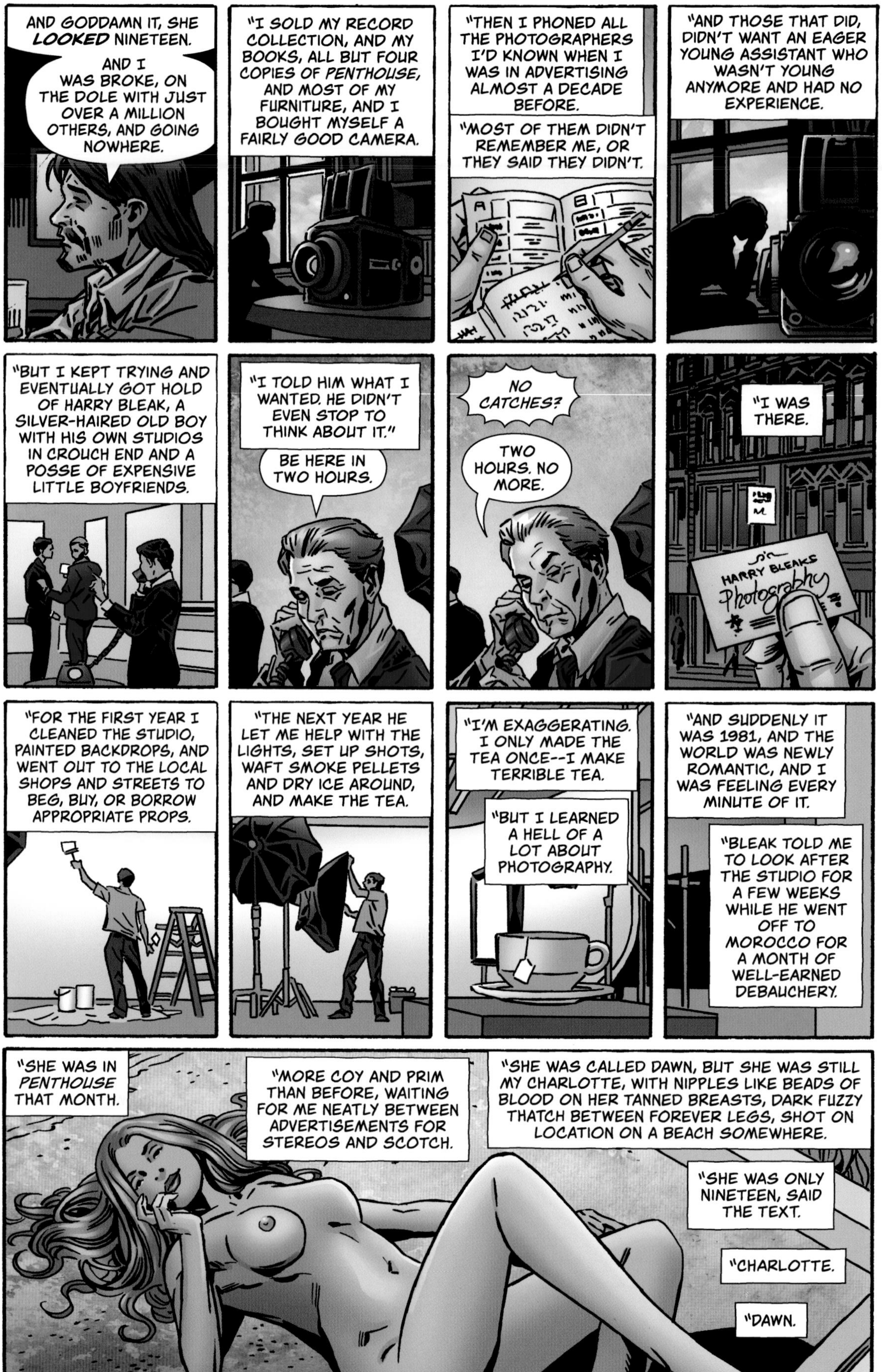
AND GODDAMN IT, SHE *LOOKED* NINETEEN.
AND I WAS BROKE, ON THE DOLE WITH JUST OVER A MILLION OTHERS, AND GOING NOWHERE.
"I SOLD MY RECORD COLLECTION, AND MY BOOKS, ALL BUT FOUR COPIES OF *PENTHOUSE*, AND MOST OF MY FURNITURE, AND I BOUGHT MYSELF A FAIRLY GOOD CAMERA.
"THEN I PHONED ALL THE PHOTOGRAPHERS I'D KNOWN WHEN I WAS IN ADVERTISING ALMOST A DECADE BEFORE.
"MOST OF THEM DIDN'T REMEMBER ME, OR THEY SAID THEY DIDN'T.
"AND THOSE THAT DID, DIDN'T WANT AN EAGER YOUNG ASSISTANT WHO WASN'T YOUNG ANYMORE AND HAD NO EXPERIENCE.
"BUT I KEPT TRYING AND EVENTUALLY GOT HOLD OF HARRY BLEAK, A SILVER-HAIRED OLD BOY WITH HIS OWN STUDIOS IN CROUCH END AND A POSSE OF EXPENSIVE LITTLE BOYFRIENDS.
"I TOLD HIM WHAT I WANTED. HE DIDN'T EVEN STOP TO THINK ABOUT IT."
BE HERE IN TWO HOURS.
NO CATCHES?
TWO HOURS. NO MORE.
"I WAS THERE.
HARRY BLEAKS
Photography
"FOR THE FIRST YEAR I CLEANED THE STUDIO, PAINTED BACKDROPS, AND WENT OUT TO THE LOCAL SHOPS AND STREETS TO BEG, BUY, OR BORROW APPROPRIATE PROPS.
"THE NEXT YEAR HE LET ME HELP WITH THE LIGHTS, SET UP SHOTS, WAFT SMOKE PELLETS AND DRY ICE AROUND, AND MAKE THE TEA.
"I'M EXAGGERATING. I ONLY MADE THE TEA ONCE--I MAKE TERRIBLE TEA.
"BUT I LEARNED A HELL OF A LOT ABOUT PHOTOGRAPHY.
"AND SUDDENLY IT WAS 1981, AND THE WORLD WAS NEWLY ROMANTIC, AND I WAS FEELING EVERY MINUTE OF IT.
"BLEAK TOLD ME TO LOOK AFTER THE STUDIO FOR A FEW WEEKS WHILE HE WENT OFF TO MOROCCO FOR A MONTH OF WELL-EARNED DEBAUCHERY.
"SHE WAS IN *PENTHOUSE* THAT MONTH.
"MORE COY AND PRIM THAN BEFORE, WAITING FOR ME NEATLY BETWEEN ADVERTISEMENTS FOR STEREOS AND SCOTCH.
"SHE WAS CALLED DAWN, BUT SHE WAS STILL MY CHARLOTTE, WITH NIPPLES LIKE BEADS OF BLOOD ON HER TANNED BREASTS, DARK FUZZY THATCH BETWEEN FOREVER LEGS, SHOT ON LOCATION ON A BEACH SOMEWHERE.
"SHE WAS ONLY NINETEEN, SAID THE TEXT.
"CHARLOTTE.
"DAWN.

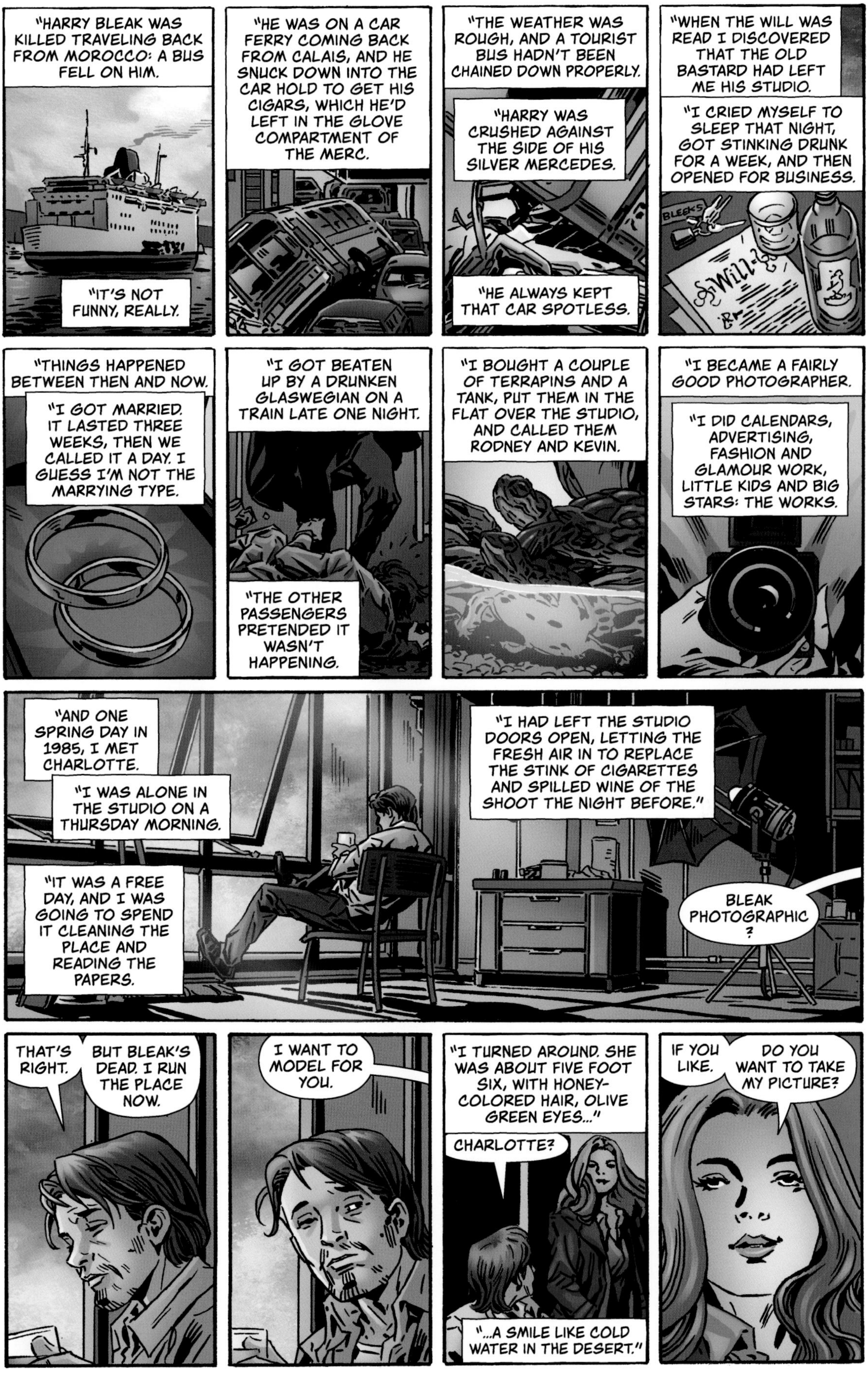
"HARRY BLEAK WAS KILLED TRAVELING BACK FROM MOROCCO: A BUS FELL ON HIM.
"IT'S NOT FUNNY, REALLY.
"HE WAS ON A CAR FERRY COMING BACK FROM CALAIS, AND HE SNUCK DOWN INTO THE CAR HOLD TO GET HIS CIGARS, WHICH HE'D LEFT IN THE GLOVE COMPARTMENT OF THE MERC.
"THE WEATHER WAS ROUGH, AND A TOURIST BUS HADN'T BEEN CHAINED DOWN PROPERLY.
"HARRY WAS CRUSHED AGAINST THE SIDE OF HIS SILVER MERCEDES.
"HE ALWAYS KEPT THAT CAR SPOTLESS.
"WHEN THE WILL WAS READ I DISCOVERED THAT THE OLD BASTARD HAD LEFT ME HIS STUDIO.
"I CRIED MYSELF TO SLEEP THAT NIGHT, GOT STINKING DRUNK FOR A WEEK, AND THEN OPENED FOR BUSINESS.
BLEEKS
Will
"THINGS HAPPENED BETWEEN THEN AND NOW.
"I GOT MARRIED. IT LASTED THREE WEEKS, THEN WE CALLED IT A DAY. I GUESS I'M NOT THE MARRYING TYPE.
"I GOT BEATEN UP BY A DRUNKEN GLASWEGIAN ON A TRAIN LATE ONE NIGHT.
"THE OTHER PASSENGERS PRETENDED IT WASN'T HAPPENING.
"I BOUGHT A COUPLE OF TERRAPINS AND A TANK, PUT THEM IN THE FLAT OVER THE STUDIO, AND CALLED THEM RODNEY AND KEVIN.
"I BECAME A FAIRLY GOOD PHOTOGRAPHER.
"I DID CALENDARS, ADVERTISING, FASHION AND GLAMOUR WORK, LITTLE KIDS AND BIG STARS: THE WORKS.
"AND ONE SPRING DAY IN 1985, I MET CHARLOTTE.
"I WAS ALONE IN THE STUDIO ON A THURSDAY MORNING.
"IT WAS A FREE DAY, AND I WAS GOING TO SPEND IT CLEANING THE PLACE AND READING THE PAPERS.
"I HAD LEFT THE STUDIO DOORS OPEN, LETTING THE FRESH AIR IN TO REPLACE THE STINK OF CIGARETTES AND SPILLED WINE OF THE SHOOT THE NIGHT BEFORE."
BLEAK PHOTOGRAPHIC?
THAT'S RIGHT.
BUT BLEAK'S DEAD. I RUN THE PLACE NOW.
I WANT TO MODEL FOR YOU.
"I TURNED AROUND. SHE WAS ABOUT FIVE FOOT SIX, WITH HONEY-COLORED HAIR, OLIVE GREEN EYES..."
CHARLOTTE?
"...A SMILE LIKE COLD WATER IN THE DESERT."
IF YOU LIKE.
DO YOU WANT TO TAKE MY PICTURE?

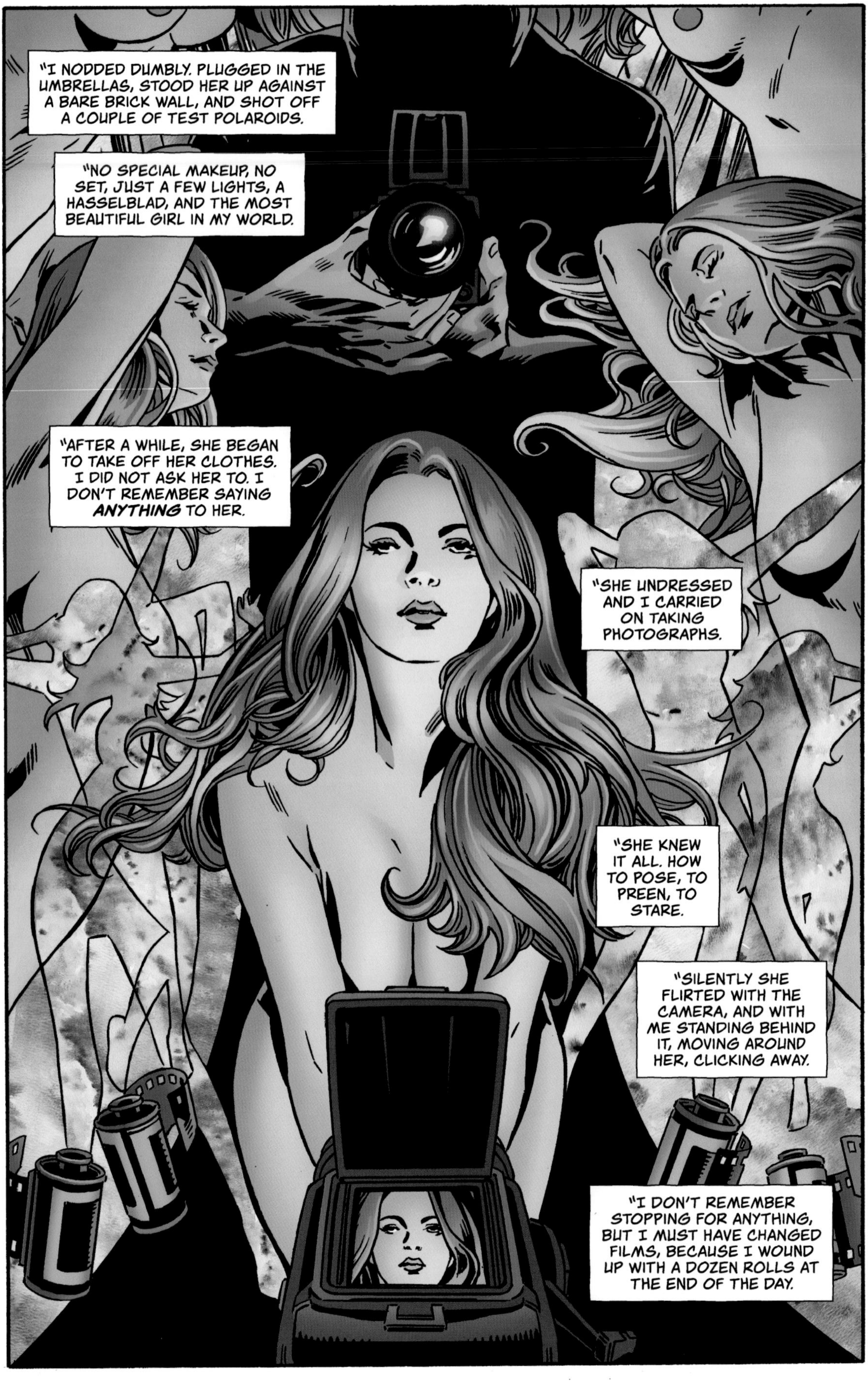
"I NODDED DUMBLY. PLUGGED IN THE UMBRELLAS, STOOD HER UP AGAINST A BARE BRICK WALL, AND SHOT OFF A COUPLE OF TEST POLAROIDS.
"NO SPECIAL MAKEUP, NO SET, JUST A FEW LIGHTS, A HASSELBLAD, AND THE MOST BEAUTIFUL GIRL IN MY WORLD.
"AFTER A WHILE, SHE BEGAN TO TAKE OFF HER CLOTHES. I DID NOT ASK HER TO. I DON'T REMEMBER SAYING *ANYTHING* TO HER.
"SHE UNDRESSED AND I CARRIED ON TAKING PHOTOGRAPHS.
"SHE KNEW IT ALL. HOW TO POSE, TO PREEN, TO STARE.
"SILENTLY SHE FLIRTED WITH THE CAMERA, AND WITH ME STANDING BEHIND IT, MOVING AROUND HER, CLICKING AWAY.
"I DON'T REMEMBER STOPPING FOR ANYTHING, BUT I MUST HAVE CHANGED FILMS, BECAUSE I WOUND UP WITH A DOZEN ROLLS AT THE END OF THE DAY.

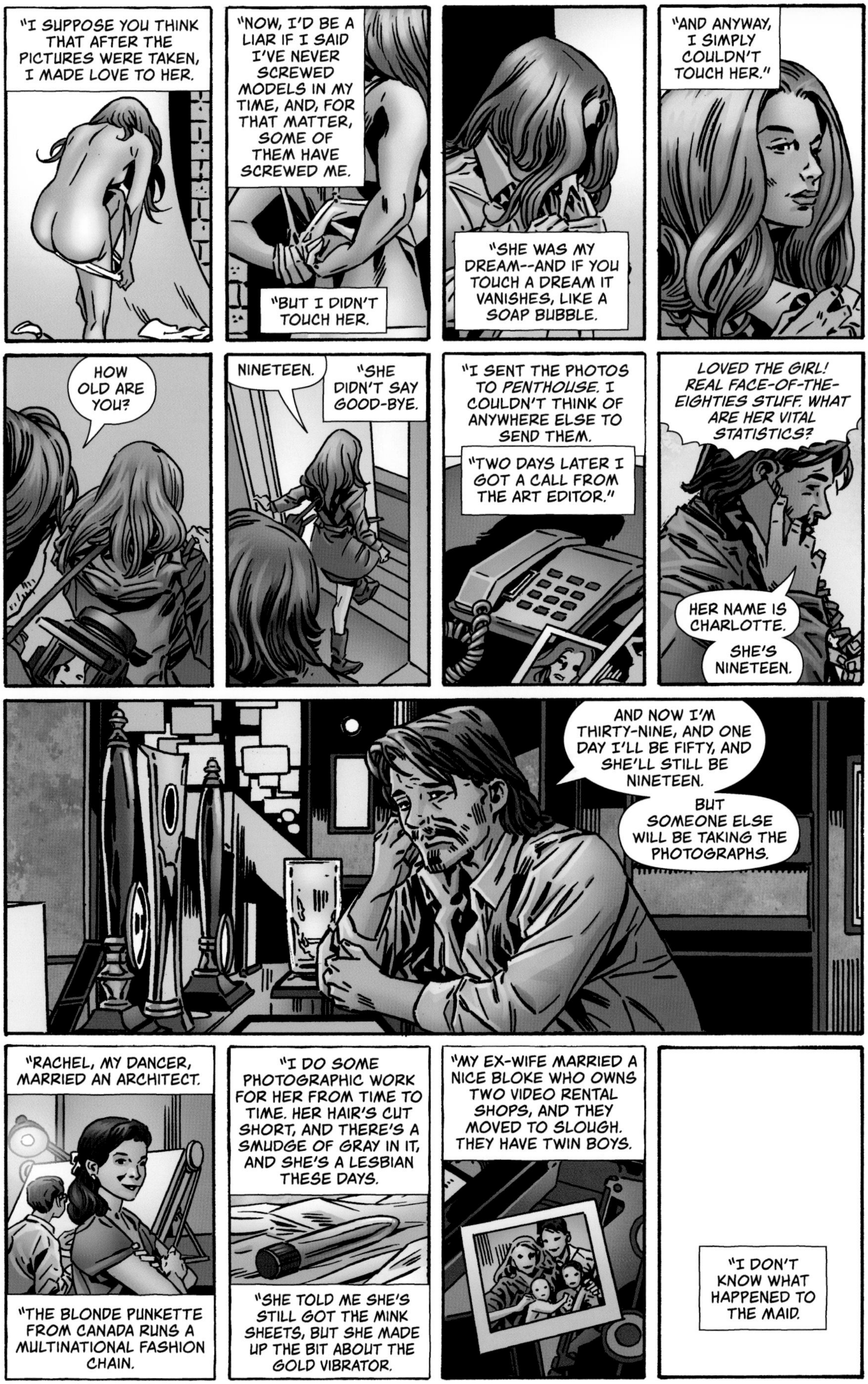
"I SUPPOSE YOU THINK THAT AFTER THE PICTURES WERE TAKEN, I MADE LOVE TO HER.
"NOW, I'D BE A LIAR IF I SAID I'VE NEVER SCREWED MODELS IN MY TIME, AND, FOR THAT MATTER, SOME OF THEM HAVE SCREWED ME.
"BUT I DIDN'T TOUCH HER.
"SHE WAS MY DREAM--AND IF YOU TOUCH A DREAM IT VANISHES, LIKE A SOAP BUBBLE.
"AND ANYWAY, I SIMPLY COULDN'T TOUCH HER."
HOW OLD ARE YOU?
NINETEEN.
"SHE DIDN'T SAY GOOD-BYE.
"I SENT THE PHOTOS TO *PENTHOUSE*. I COULDN'T THINK OF ANYWHERE ELSE TO SEND THEM.
"TWO DAYS LATER I GOT A CALL FROM THE ART EDITOR."
LOVED THE GIRL! REAL FACE-OF-THE-EIGHTIES STUFF. WHAT ARE HER VITAL STATISTICS?
HER NAME IS CHARLOTTE.
SHE'S NINETEEN.
AND NOW I'M THIRTY-NINE, AND ONE DAY I'LL BE FIFTY, AND SHE'LL STILL BE NINETEEN.
BUT SOMEONE ELSE WILL BE TAKING THE PHOTOGRAPHS.
"RACHEL, MY DANCER, MARRIED AN ARCHITECT.
"THE BLONDE PUNKETTE FROM CANADA RUNS A MULTINATIONAL FASHION CHAIN.
"I DO SOME PHOTOGRAPHIC WORK FOR HER FROM TIME TO TIME. HER HAIR'S CUT SHORT, AND THERE'S A SMUDGE OF GRAY IN IT, AND SHE'S A LESBIAN THESE DAYS.
"SHE TOLD ME SHE'S STILL GOT THE MINK SHEETS, BUT SHE MADE UP THE BIT ABOUT THE GOLD VIBRATOR.
"MY EX-WIFE MARRIED A NICE BLOKE WHO OWNS TWO VIDEO RENTAL SHOPS, AND THEY MOVED TO SLOUGH. THEY HAVE TWIN BOYS.
"I DON'T KNOW WHAT HAPPENED TO THE MAID.

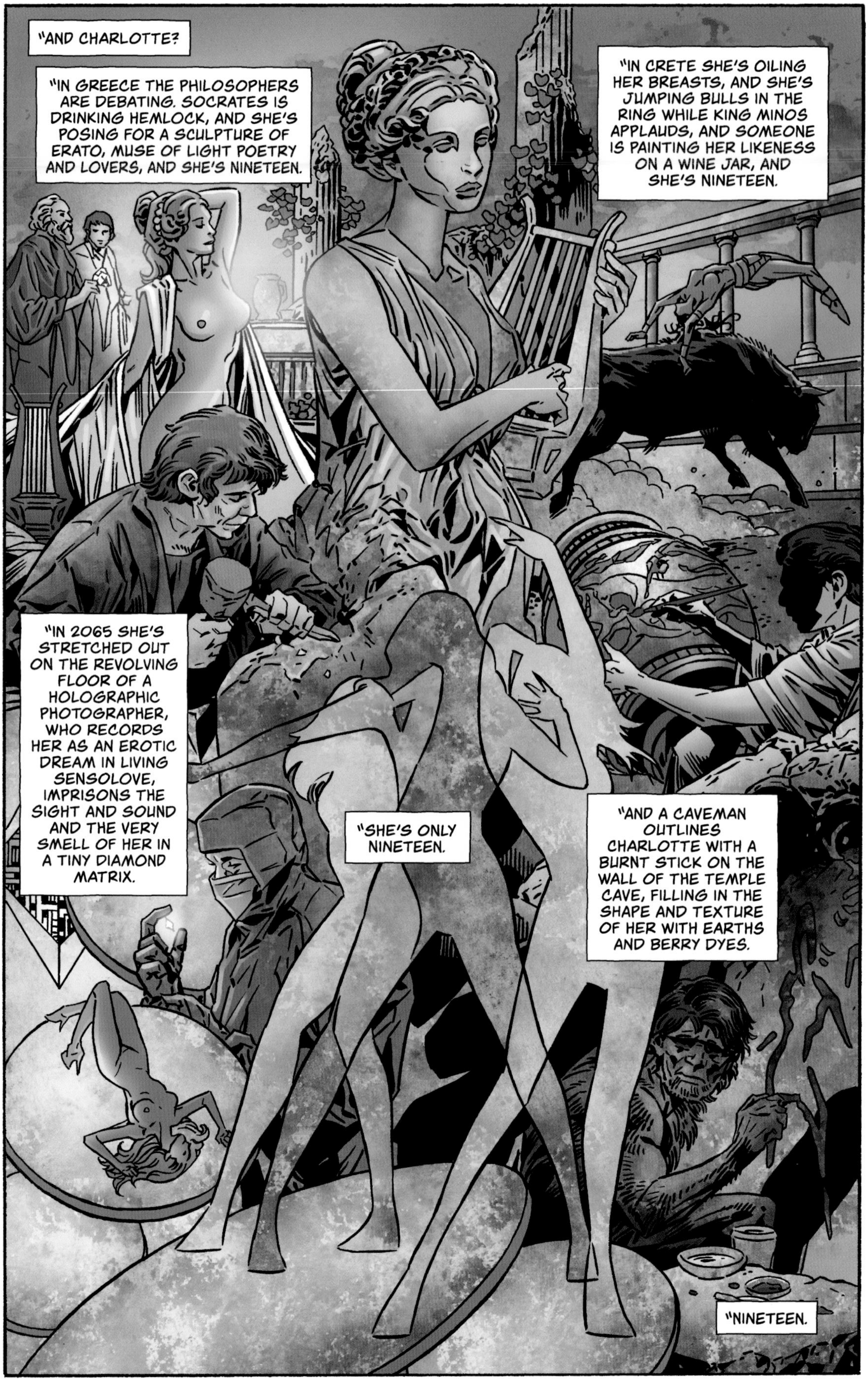
"AND CHARLOTTE?
"IN GREECE THE PHILOSOPHERS ARE DEBATING. SOCRATES IS DRINKING HEMLOCK, AND SHE'S POSING FOR A SCULPTURE OF ERATO, MUSE OF LIGHT POETRY AND LOVERS, AND SHE'S NINETEEN.
"IN CRETE SHE'S OILING HER BREASTS, AND SHE'S JUMPING BULLS IN THE RING WHILE KING MINOS APPLAUDS, AND SOMEONE IS PAINTING HER LIKENESS ON A WINE JAR, AND SHE'S NINETEEN.
"IN 2065 SHE'S STRETCHED OUT ON THE REVOLVING FLOOR OF A HOLOGRAPHIC PHOTOGRAPHER, WHO RECORDS HER AS AN EROTIC DREAM IN LIVING SENSOLOVE, IMPRISONS THE SIGHT AND SOUND AND THE VERY SMELL OF HER IN A TINY DIAMOND MATRIX.
"SHE'S ONLY NINETEEN.
"AND A CAVEMAN OUTLINES CHARLOTTE WITH A BURNT STICK ON THE WALL OF THE TEMPLE CAVE, FILLING IN THE SHAPE AND TEXTURE OF HER WITH EARTHS AND BERRY DYES.
"NINETEEN.

"CHARLOTTE IS THERE, IN ALL PLACES, ALL TIMES, SLIDING THROUGH OUR FANTASIES, A GIRL FOREVER."

I WANT HER SO MUCH IT MAKES ME HURT SOMETIMES.

"THAT'S WHEN I TAKE DOWN THE PHOTOGRAPHS OF HER AND JUST LOOK AT THEM FOR A WHILE.

"WONDERING WHY I DIDN'T TRY TO TOUCH HER.

"WHY I WOULDN'T REALLY EVEN SPEAK TO HER WHEN SHE WAS THERE, AND NEVER COMING UP WITH AN ANSWER THAT I COULD UNDERSTAND."

THIS MORNING I NOTICED YET ANOTHER GRAY HAIR AT MY TEMPLE.

CHARLOTTE IS NINETEEN.

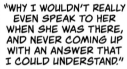

SOMEWHERE.

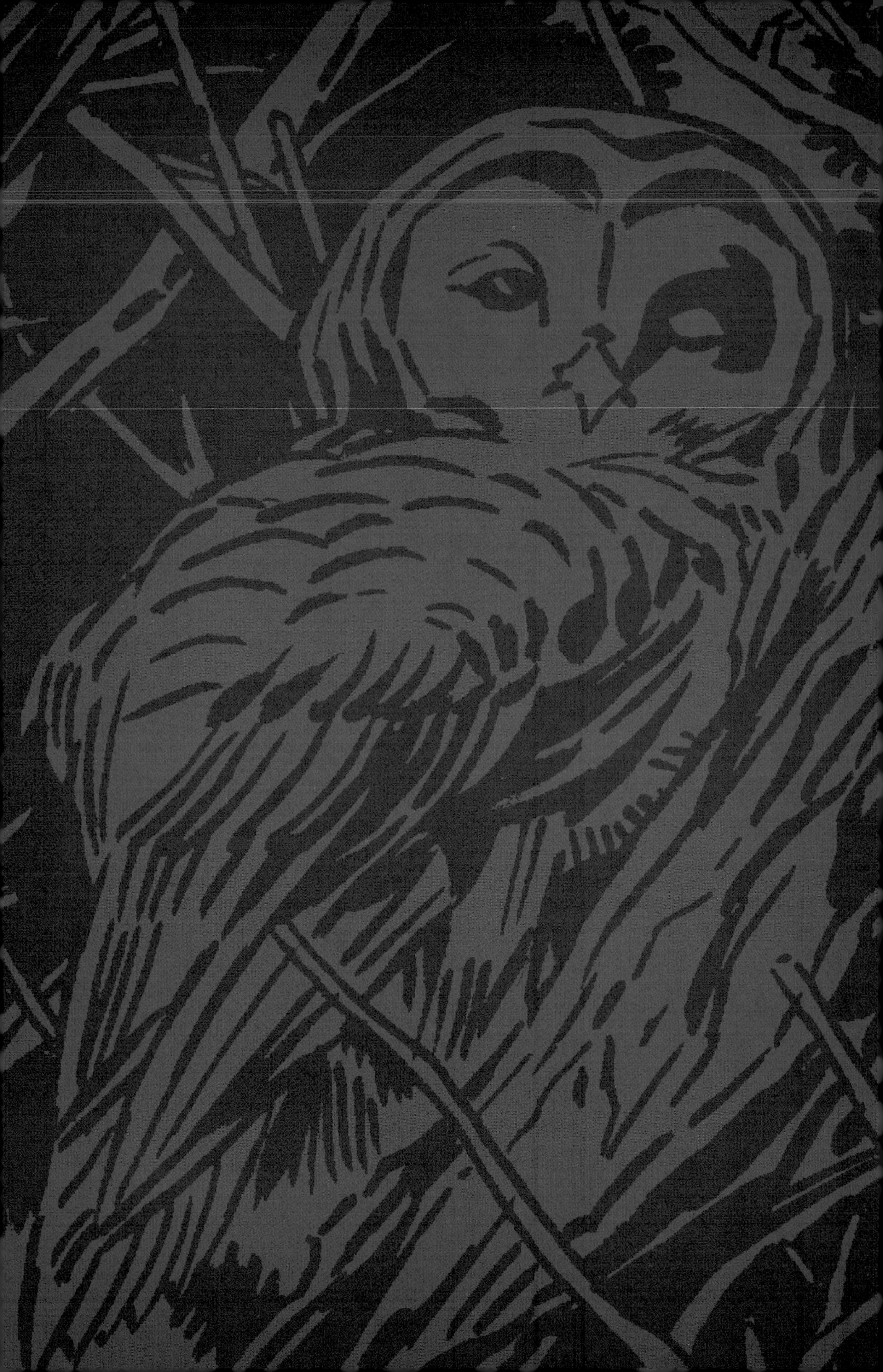

CLOSING
TIME

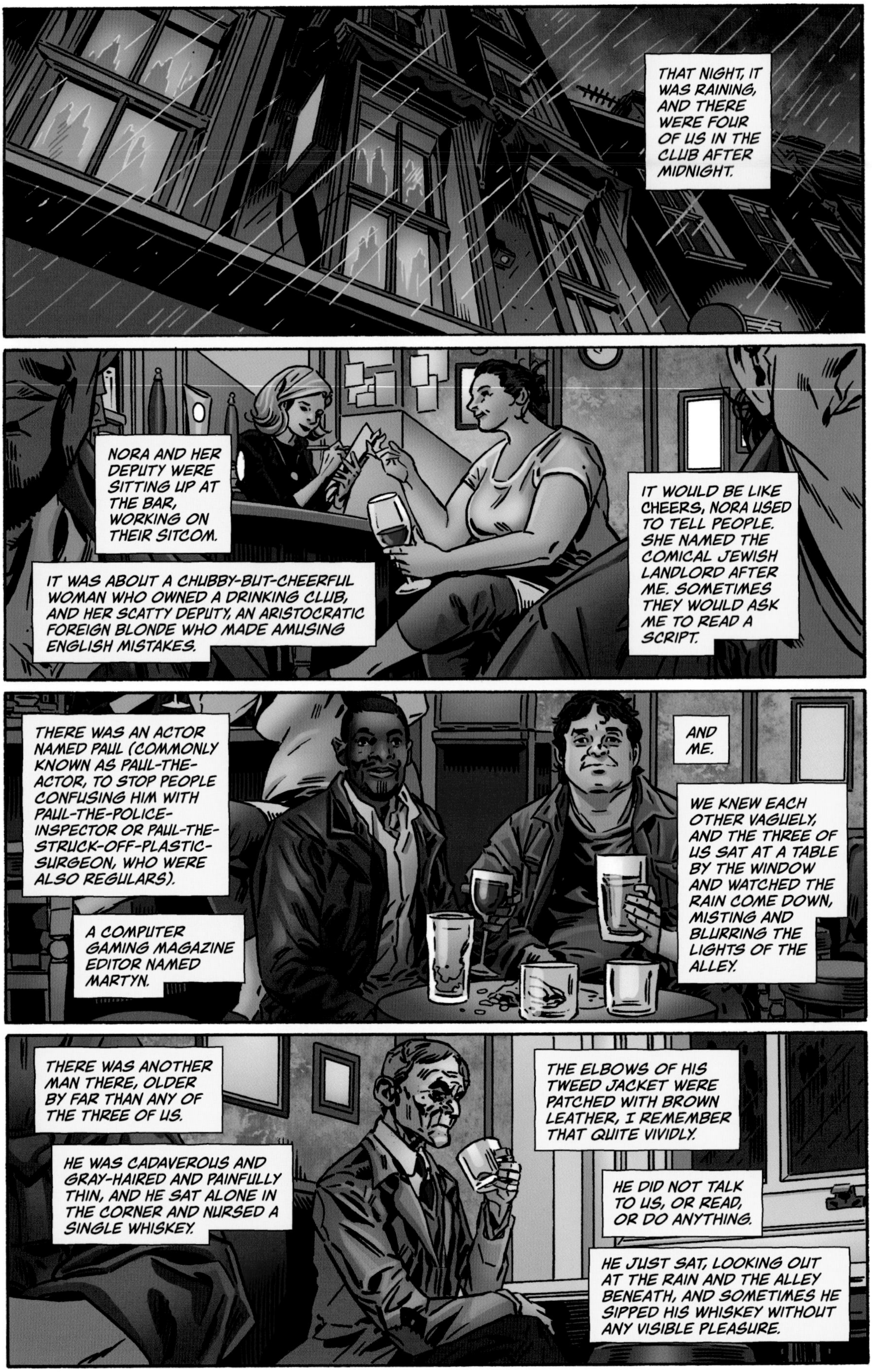
THAT NIGHT, IT WAS RAINING, AND THERE WERE FOUR OF US IN THE CLUB AFTER MIDNIGHT.
NORA AND HER DEPUTY WERE SITTING UP AT THE BAR, WORKING ON THEIR SITCOM.
IT WAS ABOUT A CHUBBY-BUT-CHEERFUL WOMAN WHO OWNED A DRINKING CLUB, AND HER SCATTY DEPUTY, AN ARISTOCRATIC FOREIGN BLONDE WHO MADE AMUSING ENGLISH MISTAKES.
IT WOULD BE LIKE CHEERS, NORA USED TO TELL PEOPLE. SHE NAMED THE COMICAL JEWISH LANDLORD AFTER ME. SOMETIMES THEY WOULD ASK ME TO READ A SCRIPT.
THERE WAS AN ACTOR NAMED PAUL (COMMONLY KNOWN AS PAUL-THE-ACTOR, TO STOP PEOPLE CONFUSING HIM WITH PAUL-THE-POLICE-INSPECTOR OR PAUL-THE-STRUCK-OFF-PLASTIC-SURGEON, WHO WERE ALSO REGULARS).
A COMPUTER GAMING MAGAZINE EDITOR NAMED MARTYN.
AND ME.
WE KNEW EACH OTHER VAGUELY, AND THE THREE OF US SAT AT A TABLE BY THE WINDOW AND WATCHED THE RAIN COME DOWN, MISTING AND BLURRING THE LIGHTS OF THE ALLEY.
THERE WAS ANOTHER MAN THERE, OLDER BY FAR THAN ANY OF THE THREE OF US.
HE WAS CADAVEROUS AND GRAY-HAIRED AND PAINFULLY THIN, AND HE SAT ALONE IN THE CORNER AND NURSED A SINGLE WHISKEY.
THE ELBOWS OF HIS TWEED JACKET WERE PATCHED WITH BROWN LEATHER, I REMEMBER THAT QUITE VIVIDLY.
HE DID NOT TALK TO US, OR READ, OR DO ANYTHING.
HE JUST SAT, LOOKING OUT AT THE RAIN AND THE ALLEY BENEATH, AND SOMETIMES HE SIPPED HIS WHISKEY WITHOUT ANY VISIBLE PLEASURE.

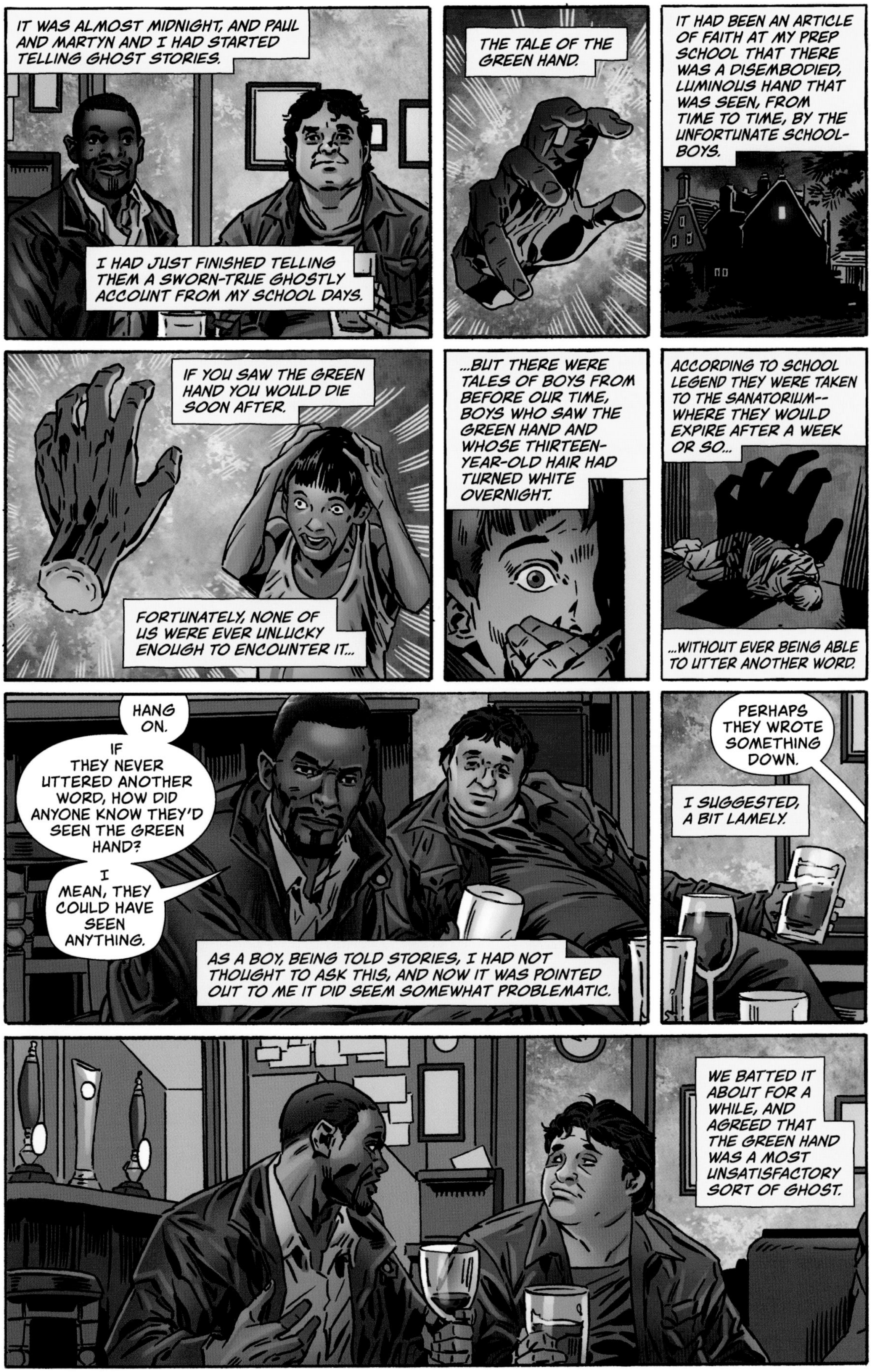
IT WAS ALMOST MIDNIGHT, AND PAUL AND MARTYN AND I HAD STARTED TELLING GHOST STORIES.
I HAD JUST FINISHED TELLING THEM A SWORN-TRUE GHOSTLY ACCOUNT FROM MY SCHOOL DAYS.
THE TALE OF THE GREEN HAND.
IT HAD BEEN AN ARTICLE OF FAITH AT MY PREP SCHOOL THAT THERE WAS A DISEMBODIED, LUMINOUS HAND THAT WAS SEEN, FROM TIME TO TIME, BY THE UNFORTUNATE SCHOOL-BOYS.
IF YOU SAW THE GREEN HAND YOU WOULD DIE SOON AFTER.
FORTUNATELY, NONE OF US WERE EVER UNLUCKY ENOUGH TO ENCOUNTER IT...
...BUT THERE WERE TALES OF BOYS FROM BEFORE OUR TIME, BOYS WHO SAW THE GREEN HAND AND WHOSE THIRTEEN-YEAR-OLD HAIR HAD TURNED WHITE OVERNIGHT.
ACCORDING TO SCHOOL LEGEND THEY WERE TAKEN TO THE SANATORIUM--WHERE THEY WOULD EXPIRE AFTER A WEEK OR SO...
...WITHOUT EVER BEING ABLE TO UTTER ANOTHER WORD.
HANG ON.
IF THEY NEVER UTTERED ANOTHER WORD, HOW DID ANYONE KNOW THEY'D SEEN THE GREEN HAND?
I MEAN, THEY COULD HAVE SEEN ANYTHING.
AS A BOY, BEING TOLD STORIES, I HAD NOT THOUGHT TO ASK THIS, AND NOW IT WAS POINTED OUT TO ME IT DID SEEM SOMEWHAT PROBLEMATIC.
PERHAPS THEY WROTE SOMETHING DOWN.
I SUGGESTED, A BIT LAMELY.
WE BATTED IT ABOUT FOR A WHILE, AND AGREED THAT THE GREEN HAND WAS A MOST UNSATISFACTORY SORT OF GHOST.

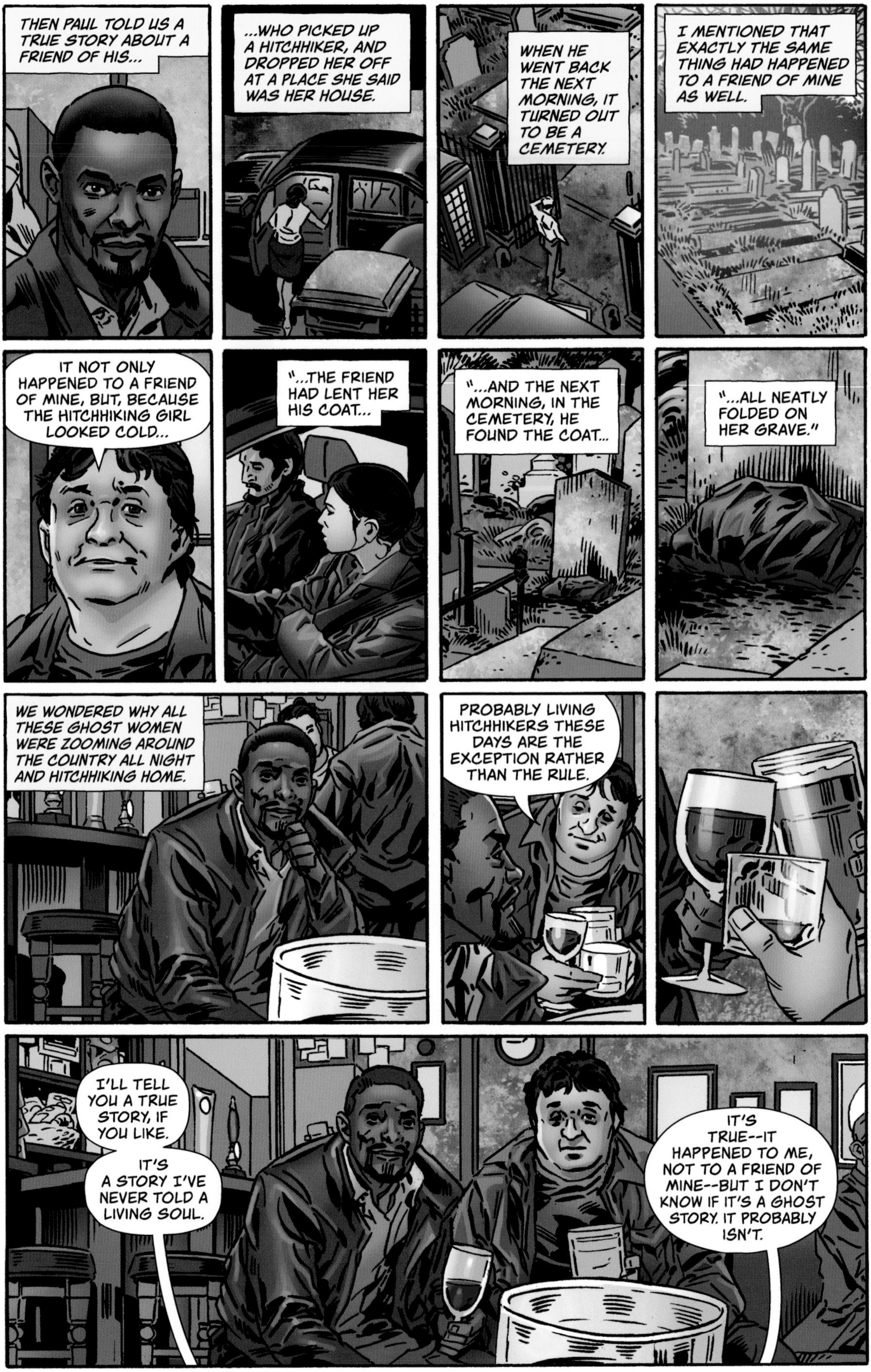

THEN PAUL TOLD US A TRUE STORY ABOUT A FRIEND OF HIS...
...WHO PICKED UP A HITCHHIKER, AND DROPPED HER OFF AT A PLACE SHE SAID WAS HER HOUSE.
WHEN HE WENT BACK THE NEXT MORNING, IT TURNED OUT TO BE A CEMETERY.
I MENTIONED THAT EXACTLY THE SAME THING HAD HAPPENED TO A FRIEND OF MINE AS WELL.
IT NOT ONLY HAPPENED TO A FRIEND OF MINE, BUT, BECAUSE THE HITCHHIKING GIRL LOOKED COLD...
"...THE FRIEND HAD LENT HER HIS COAT...
"...AND THE NEXT MORNING, IN THE CEMETERY, HE FOUND THE COAT...
"...ALL NEATLY FOLDED ON HER GRAVE."
WE WONDERED WHY ALL THESE GHOST WOMEN WERE ZOOMING AROUND THE COUNTRY ALL NIGHT AND HITCHHIKING HOME.
PROBABLY LIVING HITCHHIKERS THESE DAYS ARE THE EXCEPTION RATHER THAN THE RULE.
I'LL TELL YOU A TRUE STORY, IF YOU LIKE.
IT'S A STORY I'VE NEVER TOLD A LIVING SOUL.
IT'S TRUE--IT HAPPENED TO ME, NOT TO A FRIEND OF MINE--BUT I DON'T KNOW IF IT'S A GHOST STORY. IT PROBABLY ISN'T.

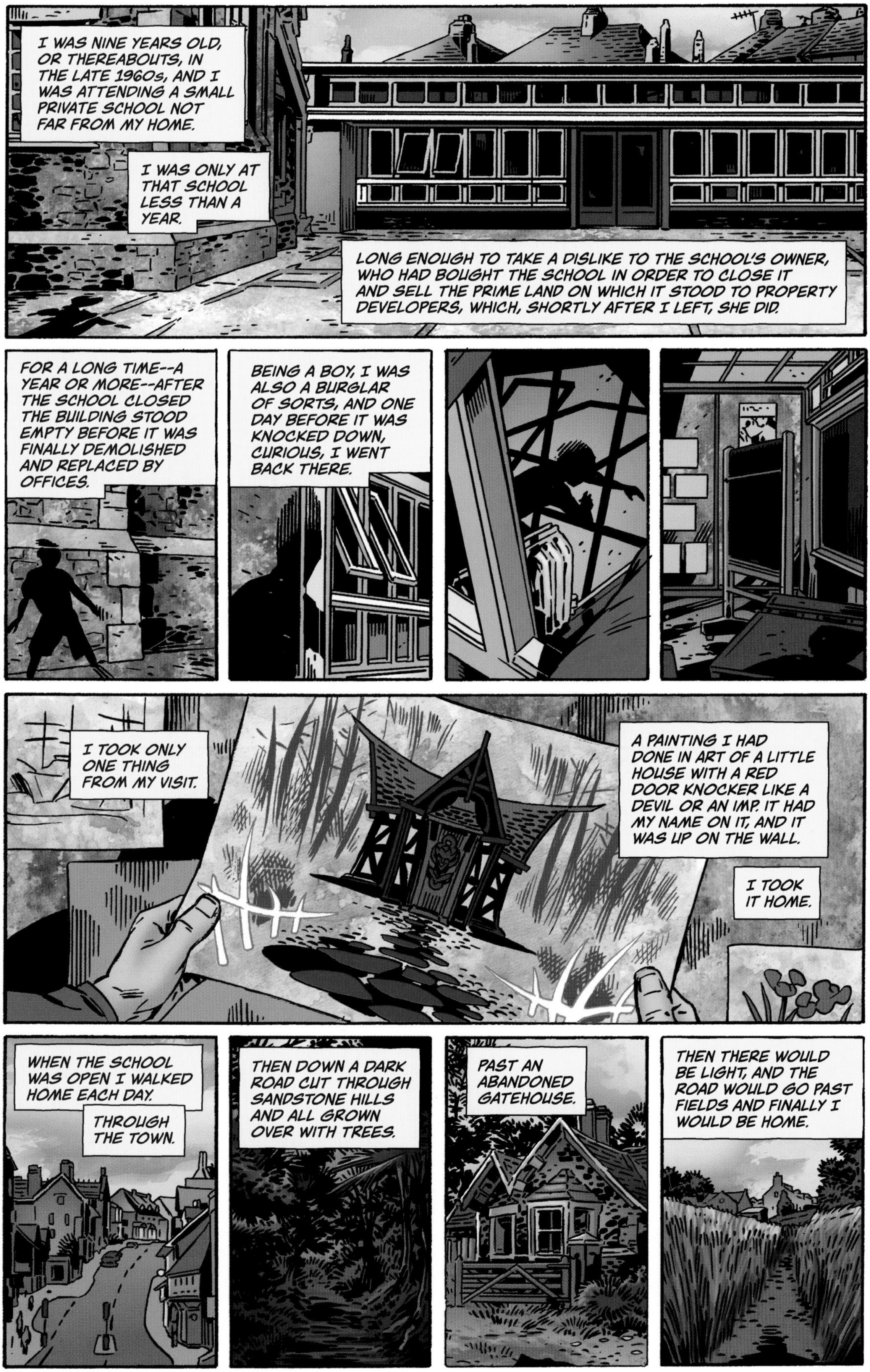

I WAS NINE YEARS OLD, OR THEREABOUTS, IN THE LATE 1960s, AND I WAS ATTENDING A SMALL PRIVATE SCHOOL NOT FAR FROM MY HOME.
I WAS ONLY AT THAT SCHOOL LESS THAN A YEAR.
LONG ENOUGH TO TAKE A DISLIKE TO THE SCHOOL'S OWNER, WHO HAD BOUGHT THE SCHOOL IN ORDER TO CLOSE IT AND SELL THE PRIME LAND ON WHICH IT STOOD TO PROPERTY DEVELOPERS, WHICH, SHORTLY AFTER I LEFT, SHE DID.
FOR A LONG TIME--A YEAR OR MORE--AFTER THE SCHOOL CLOSED THE BUILDING STOOD EMPTY BEFORE IT WAS FINALLY DEMOLISHED AND REPLACED BY OFFICES.
BEING A BOY, I WAS ALSO A BURGLAR OF SORTS, AND ONE DAY BEFORE IT WAS KNOCKED DOWN, CURIOUS, I WENT BACK THERE.
I TOOK ONLY ONE THING FROM MY VISIT.
A PAINTING I HAD DONE IN ART OF A LITTLE HOUSE WITH A RED DOOR KNOCKER LIKE A DEVIL OR AN IMP. IT HAD MY NAME ON IT, AND IT WAS UP ON THE WALL.
I TOOK IT HOME.
WHEN THE SCHOOL WAS OPEN I WALKED HOME EACH DAY.
THROUGH THE TOWN.
THEN DOWN A DARK ROAD CUT THROUGH SANDSTONE HILLS AND ALL GROWN OVER WITH TREES.
PAST AN ABANDONED GATEHOUSE.
THEN THERE WOULD BE LIGHT, AND THE ROAD WOULD GO PAST FIELDS AND FINALLY I WOULD BE HOME.

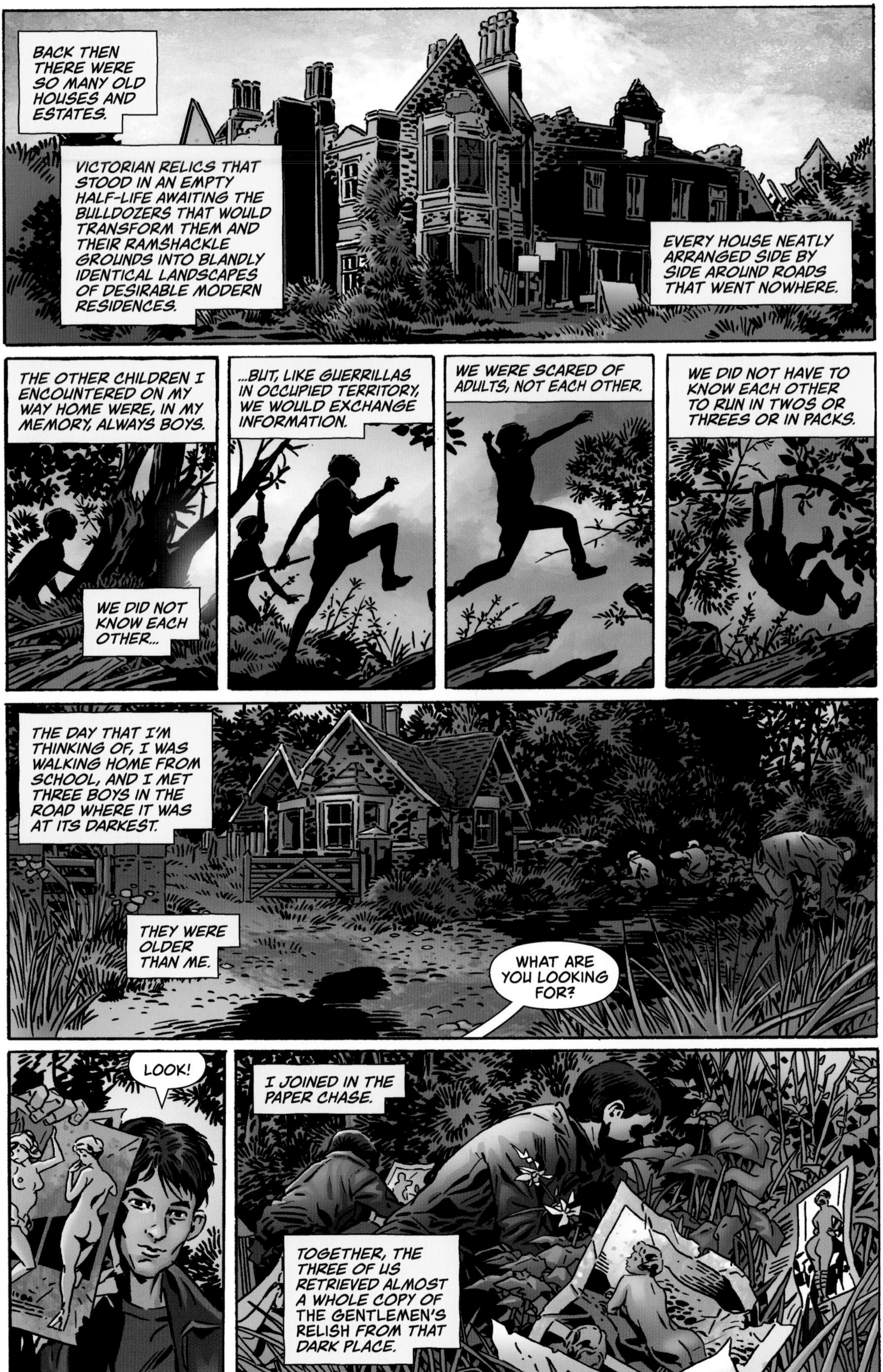
BACK THEN THERE WERE SO MANY OLD HOUSES AND ESTATES.
VICTORIAN RELICS THAT STOOD IN AN EMPTY HALF-LIFE AWAITING THE BULLDOZERS THAT WOULD TRANSFORM THEM AND THEIR RAMSHACKLE GROUNDS INTO BLANDLY IDENTICAL LANDSCAPES OF DESIRABLE MODERN RESIDENCES.
EVERY HOUSE NEATLY ARRANGED SIDE BY SIDE AROUND ROADS THAT WENT NOWHERE.
THE OTHER CHILDREN I ENCOUNTERED ON MY WAY HOME WERE, IN MY MEMORY, ALWAYS BOYS.
WE DID NOT KNOW EACH OTHER...
...BUT, LIKE GUERRILLAS IN OCCUPIED TERRITORY, WE WOULD EXCHANGE INFORMATION.
WE WERE SCARED OF ADULTS, NOT EACH OTHER.
WE DID NOT HAVE TO KNOW EACH OTHER TO RUN IN TWOS OR THREES OR IN PACKS.
THE DAY THAT I'M THINKING OF, I WAS WALKING HOME FROM SCHOOL, AND I MET THREE BOYS IN THE ROAD WHERE IT WAS AT ITS DARKEST.
THEY WERE OLDER THAN ME.
WHAT ARE YOU LOOKING FOR?
LOOK!
I JOINED IN THE PAPER CHASE.
TOGETHER, THE THREE OF US RETRIEVED ALMOST A WHOLE COPY OF THE GENTLEMEN'S RELISH FROM THAT DARK PLACE.

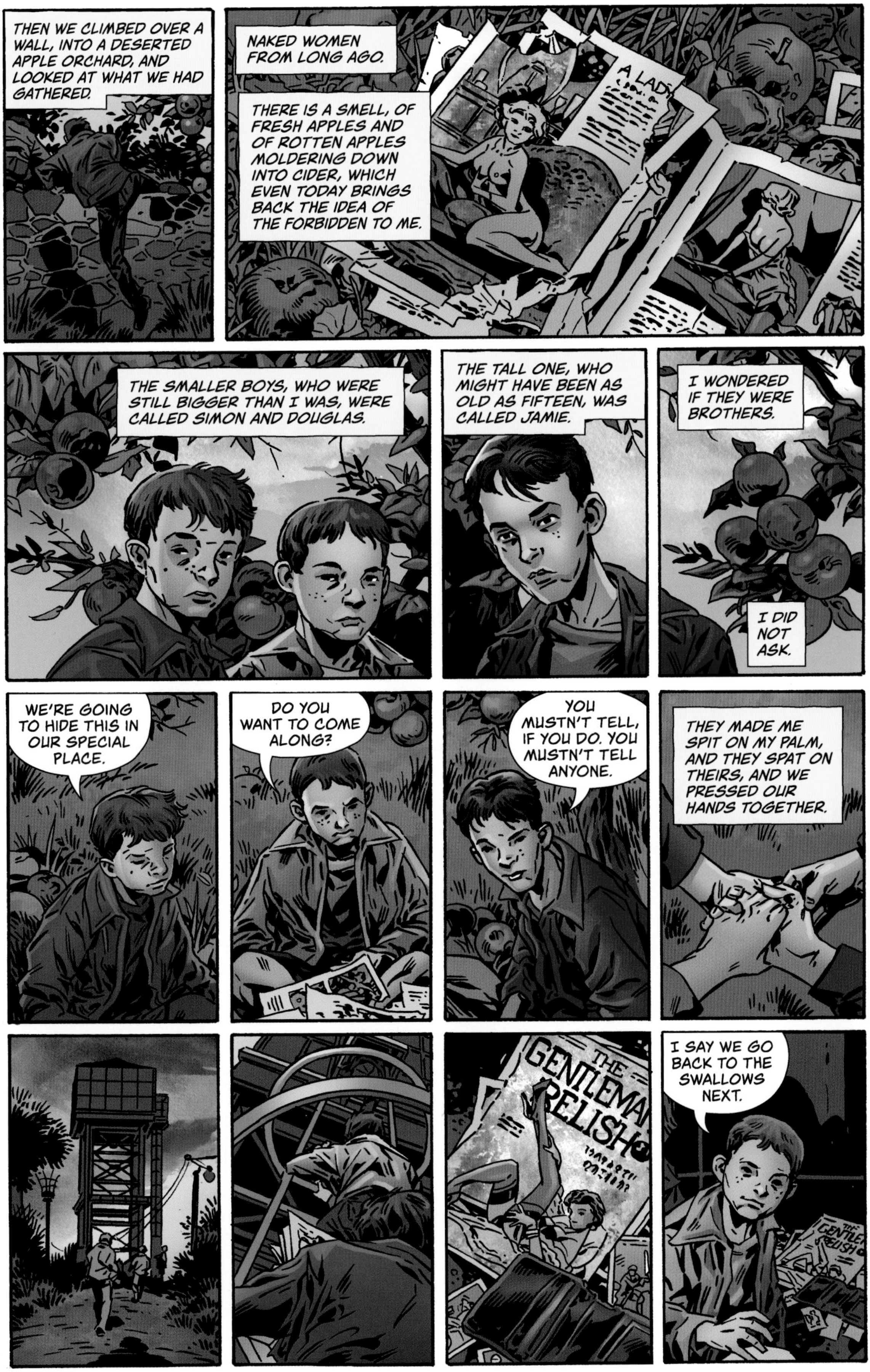
THEN WE CLIMBED OVER A WALL, INTO A DESERTED APPLE ORCHARD, AND LOOKED AT WHAT WE HAD GATHERED.
NAKED WOMEN FROM LONG AGO.
THERE IS A SMELL, OF FRESH APPLES AND OF ROTTEN APPLES MOLDERING DOWN INTO CIDER, WHICH EVEN TODAY BRINGS BACK THE IDEA OF THE FORBIDDEN TO ME.
THE SMALLER BOYS, WHO WERE STILL BIGGER THAN I WAS, WERE CALLED SIMON AND DOUGLAS.
THE TALL ONE, WHO MIGHT HAVE BEEN AS OLD AS FIFTEEN, WAS CALLED JAMIE.
I WONDERED IF THEY WERE BROTHERS.
I DID NOT ASK.
WE'RE GOING TO HIDE THIS IN OUR SPECIAL PLACE.
DO YOU WANT TO COME ALONG?
YOU MUSTN'T TELL, IF YOU DO. YOU MUSTN'T TELL ANYONE.
THEY MADE ME SPIT ON MY PALM, AND THEY SPAT ON THEIRS, AND WE PRESSED OUR HANDS TOGETHER.
I SAY WE GO BACK TO THE SWALLOWS NEXT.

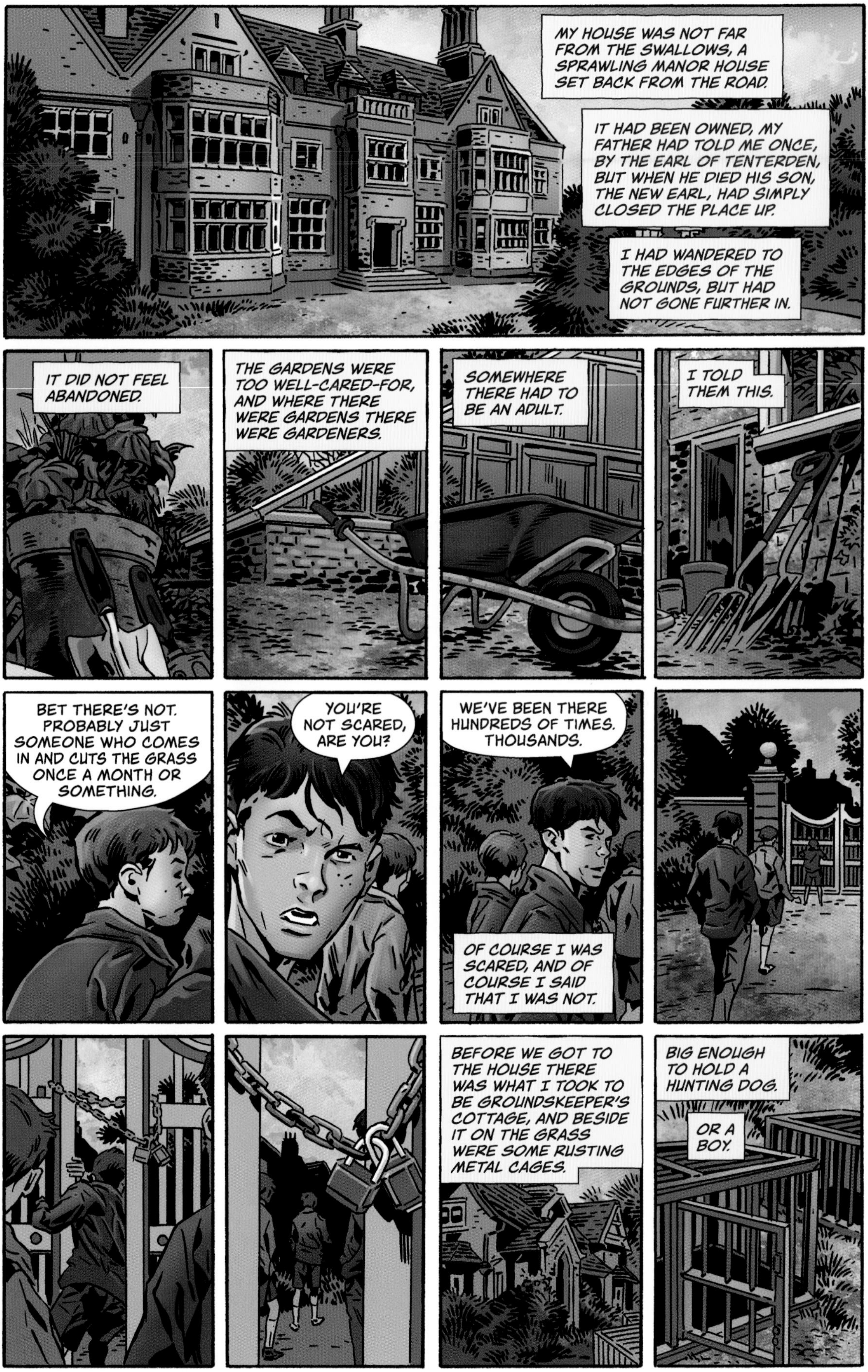
MY HOUSE WAS NOT FAR FROM THE SWALLOWS, A SPRAWLING MANOR HOUSE SET BACK FROM THE ROAD.
IT HAD BEEN OWNED, MY FATHER HAD TOLD ME ONCE, BY THE EARL OF TENTERDEN, BUT WHEN HE DIED HIS SON, THE NEW EARL, HAD SIMPLY CLOSED THE PLACE UP.
I HAD WANDERED TO THE EDGES OF THE GROUNDS, BUT HAD NOT GONE FURTHER IN.
IT DID NOT FEEL ABANDONED.
THE GARDENS WERE TOO WELL-CARED-FOR, AND WHERE THERE WERE GARDENS THERE WERE GARDENERS.
SOMEWHERE THERE HAD TO BE AN ADULT.
I TOLD THEM THIS.
BET THERE'S NOT. PROBABLY JUST SOMEONE WHO COMES IN AND CUTS THE GRASS ONCE A MONTH OR SOMETHING.
YOU'RE NOT SCARED, ARE YOU?
WE'VE BEEN THERE HUNDREDS OF TIMES. THOUSANDS.
OF COURSE I WAS SCARED, AND OF COURSE I SAID THAT I WAS NOT.
BEFORE WE GOT TO THE HOUSE THERE WAS WHAT I TOOK TO BE GROUNDSKEEPER'S COTTAGE, AND BESIDE IT ON THE GRASS WERE SOME RUSTING METAL CAGES.
BIG ENOUGH TO HOLD A HUNTING DOG.
OR A BOY.

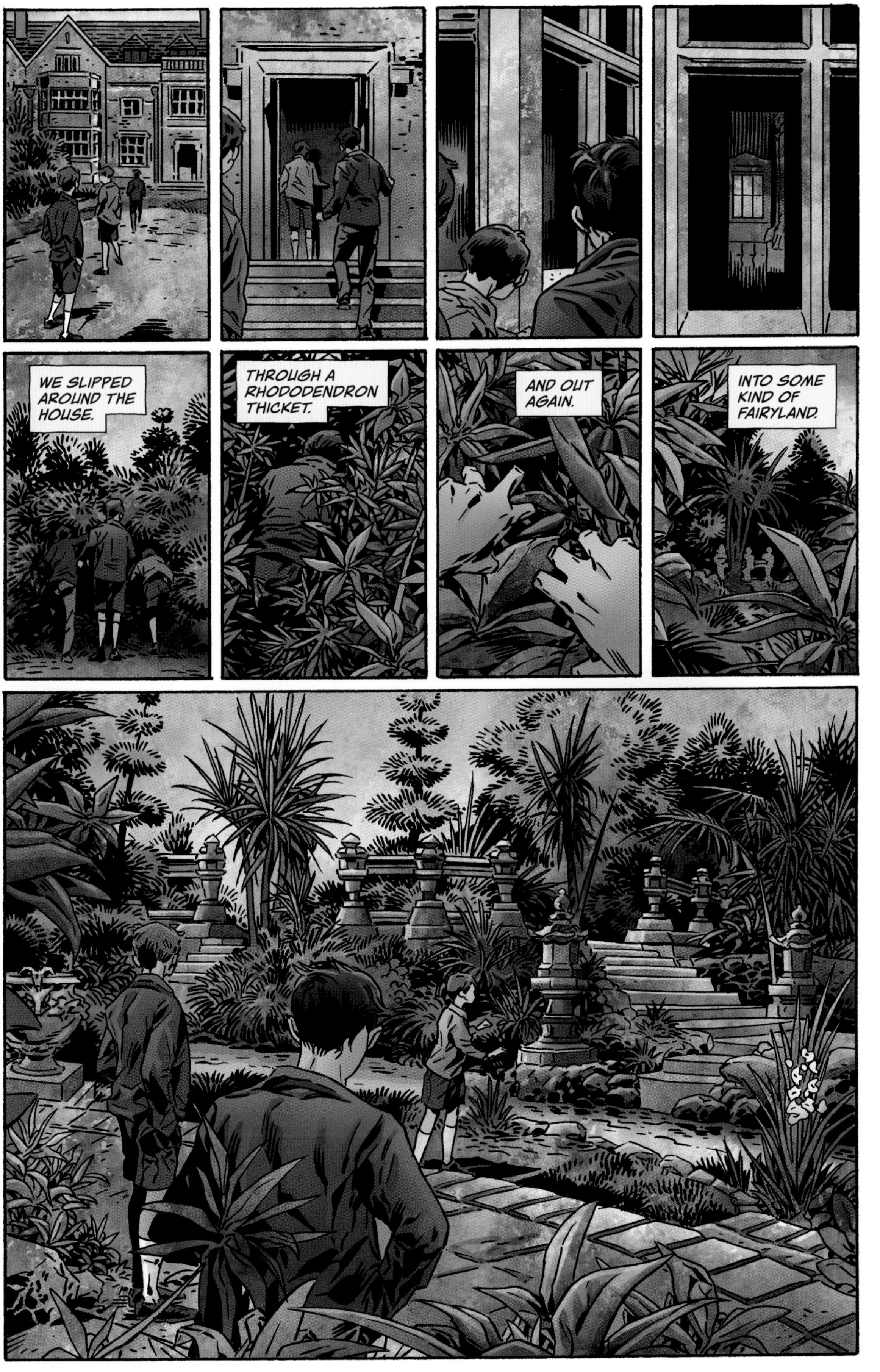
WE SLIPPED AROUND THE HOUSE.
THROUGH A RHODODENDRON THICKET.
AND OUT AGAIN.
INTO SOME KIND OF FAIRYLAND.

I'M GOING TO WEE-WEE IN IT.

I WAS SHOCKED. I REMEMBER THAT.

I SUPPOSE I WAS SHOCKED BY THE JOY THEY TOOK IN THIS...

...OR JUST BY THE WAY THEY WERE DOING SOMETHING LIKE THAT IN SUCH A SPECIAL PLACE.

SPOILING THE CLEAR WATER AND THE MAGIC OF THE PLACE.

MAKING IT INTO A TOILET.

IT SEEMED WRONG.

WE'RE CAVALIERS.

DO YOU KNOW WHAT THAT MEANS?

I KNEW ABOUT THE ENGLISH CIVIL WAR, CAVALIERS (WRONG BUT ROMANTIC) VERSUS ROUNDHEADS (RIGHT BUT REPULSIVE), BUT I DIDN'T THINK THAT WAS WHAT THEY WERE TALKING ABOUT.

I SHOOK MY HEAD.

IT MEANS OUR WILLIES AREN'T CIRCUMCISED.

ARE YOU A CAVALIER OR A ROUNDHEAD?

I KNEW WHAT THEY MEANT NOW.

I'M A ROUNDHEAD.

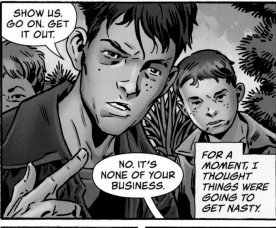
SHOW US. GO ON. GET IT OUT.

NO. IT'S NONE OF YOUR BUSINESS.

FOR A MOMENT, I THOUGHT THINGS WERE GOING TO GET NASTY.

BUT THEN JAMIE LAUGHED, AND PUT HIS PENIS AWAY, AND THE OTHERS DID THE SAME.

THEY TOLD DIRTY JOKES TO EACH OTHER THEN, JOKES I REALLY DIDN'T UNDERSTAND, FOR ALL THAT I WAS A BRIGHT CHILD.

BUT I HEARD AND REMEMBERED THEM, AND SEVERAL WEEKS LATER WAS ALMOST EXPELLED FROM SCHOOL FOR TELLING ONE OF THEM TO A BOY WHO WENT HOME AND TOLD IT TO HIS PARENTS.

THE JOKE HAD THE WORD **FUCK** IN IT.

YOU MUST NEVER, EVER SAY THAT WORD.

THAT IS THE WORST WORD ANYONE CAN SAY.

I PROMISED HER THAT I WOULDN'T.

BUT AFTER, AMAZED AT THE POWER A SINGLE WORD COULD HAVE, I WOULD WHISPER IT TO MYSELF, WHEN I WAS ALONE.

THE THREE BIG BOYS TOLD JOKES AND THEY LAUGHED AND THEY LAUGHED, AND I LAUGHED, TOO, ALTHOUGH I DID NOT UNDERSTAND ANY OF WHAT THEY WERE LAUGHING ABOUT.

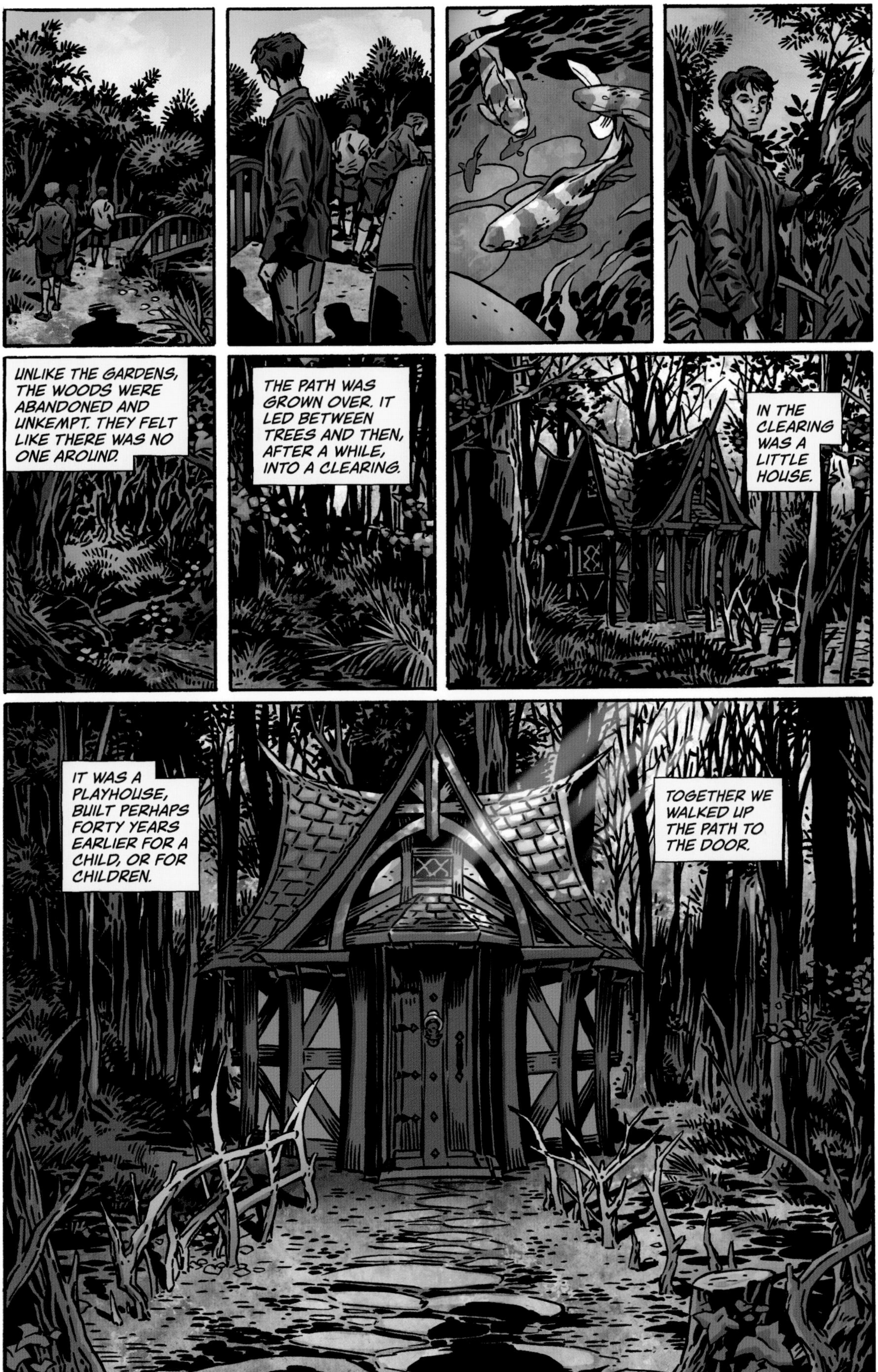
UNLIKE THE GARDENS, THE WOODS WERE ABANDONED AND UNKEMPT. THEY FELT LIKE THERE WAS NO ONE AROUND.
THE PATH WAS GROWN OVER. IT LED BETWEEN TREES AND THEN, AFTER A WHILE, INTO A CLEARING.
IN THE CLEARING WAS A LITTLE HOUSE.
IT WAS A PLAYHOUSE, BUILT PERHAPS FORTY YEARS EARLIER FOR A CHILD, OR FOR CHILDREN.
TOGETHER WE WALKED UP THE PATH TO THE DOOR.

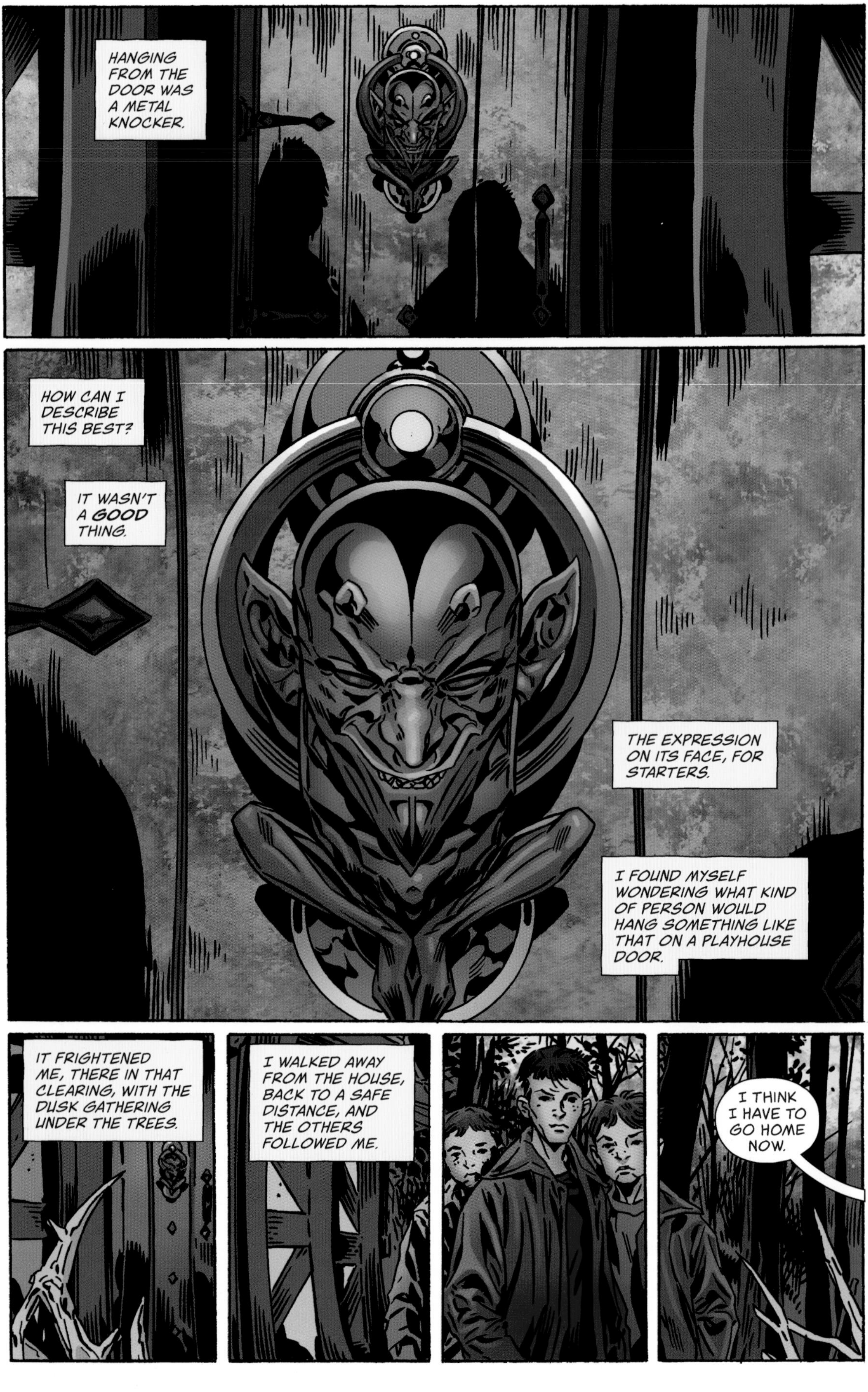
HANGING FROM THE DOOR WAS A METAL KNOCKER.
HOW CAN I DESCRIBE THIS BEST?
IT WASN'T A **GOOD** THING.
THE EXPRESSION ON ITS FACE, FOR STARTERS.
I FOUND MYSELF WONDERING WHAT KIND OF PERSON WOULD HANG SOMETHING LIKE THAT ON A PLAYHOUSE DOOR.
IT FRIGHTENED ME, THERE IN THAT CLEARING, WITH THE DUSK GATHERING UNDER THE TREES.
I WALKED AWAY FROM THE HOUSE, BACK TO A SAFE DISTANCE, AND THE OTHERS FOLLOWED ME.
I THINK I HAVE TO GO HOME NOW.

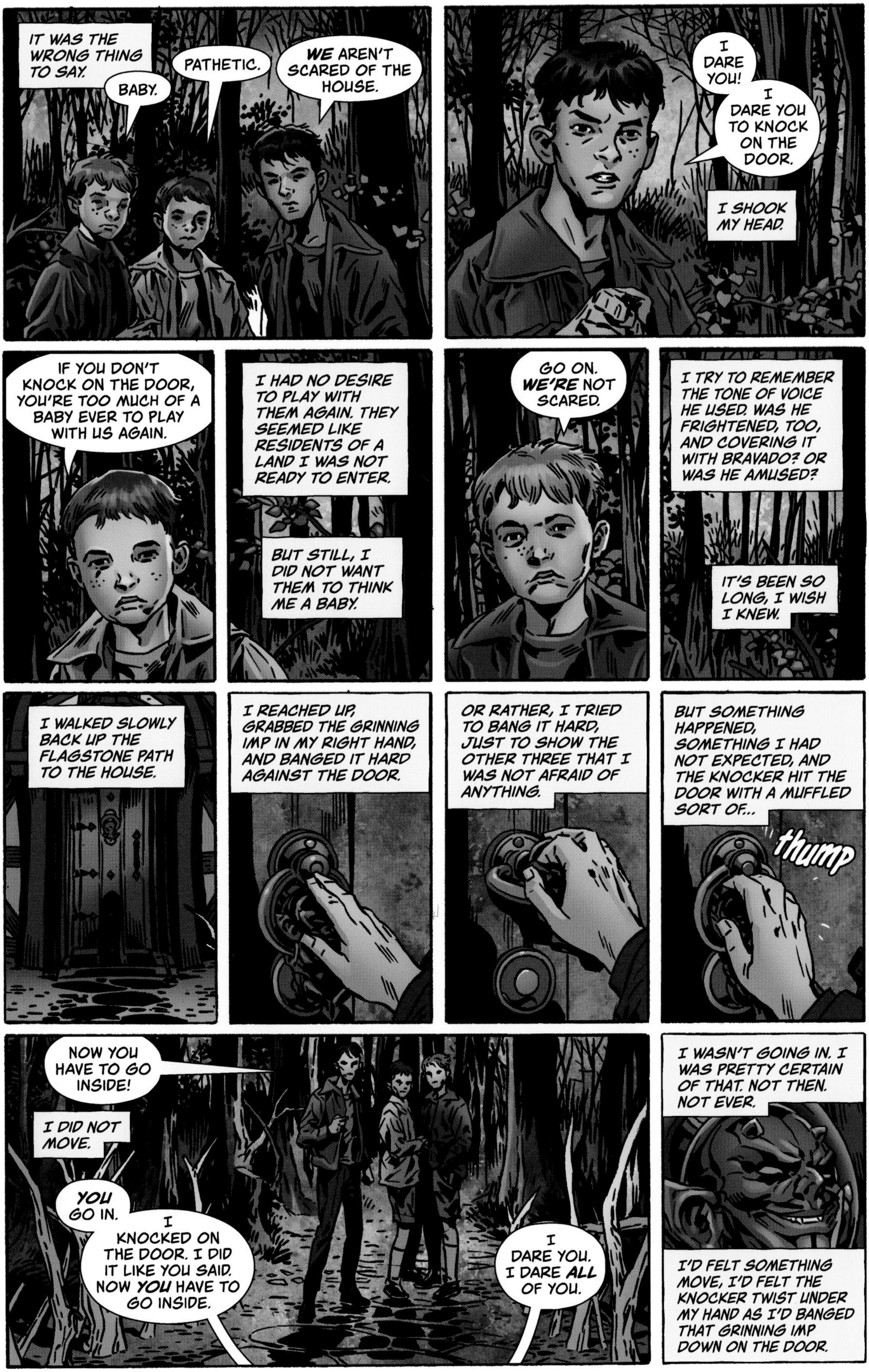
IT WAS THE WRONG THING TO SAY.
BABY.
PATHETIC.
WE AREN'T SCARED OF THE HOUSE.
I DARE YOU!
I DARE YOU TO KNOCK ON THE DOOR.
I SHOOK MY HEAD.
IF YOU DON'T KNOCK ON THE DOOR, YOU'RE TOO MUCH OF A BABY EVER TO PLAY WITH US AGAIN.
I HAD NO DESIRE TO PLAY WITH THEM AGAIN. THEY SEEMED LIKE RESIDENTS OF A LAND I WAS NOT READY TO ENTER.
BUT STILL, I DID NOT WANT THEM TO THINK ME A BABY.
GO ON. WE'RE NOT SCARED.
I TRY TO REMEMBER THE TONE OF VOICE HE USED. WAS HE FRIGHTENED, TOO, AND COVERING IT WITH BRAVADO? OR WAS HE AMUSED?
IT'S BEEN SO LONG, I WISH I KNEW.
I WALKED SLOWLY BACK UP THE FLAGSTONE PATH TO THE HOUSE.
I REACHED UP, GRABBED THE GRINNING IMP IN MY RIGHT HAND, AND BANGED IT HARD AGAINST THE DOOR.
OR RATHER, I TRIED TO BANG IT HARD, JUST TO SHOW THE OTHER THREE THAT I WAS NOT AFRAID OF ANYTHING.
BUT SOMETHING HAPPENED, SOMETHING I HAD NOT EXPECTED, AND THE KNOCKER HIT THE DOOR WITH A MUFFLED SORT OF...
thump
NOW YOU HAVE TO GO INSIDE!
I DID NOT MOVE.
YOU GO IN.
I KNOCKED ON THE DOOR. I DID IT LIKE YOU SAID. NOW YOU HAVE TO GO INSIDE.
I DARE YOU. I DARE ALL OF YOU.
I WASN'T GOING IN. I WAS PRETTY CERTAIN OF THAT. NOT THEN. NOT EVER.
I'D FELT SOMETHING MOVE, I'D FELT THE KNOCKER TWIST UNDER MY HAND AS I'D BANGED THAT GRINNING IMP DOWN ON THE DOOR.

OR ARE YOU SCARED?

IT'S GETTING DARK.

THE DOOR BANGED SHUT BEHIND THEM, AND I SWEAR TO GOD I DID NOT TOUCH IT.

I WALKED AROUND TO THE SIDE OF THE PLAYHOUSE AND PEERED THROUGH ALL THE WINDOWS, ONE BY ONE, INTO THE DARK AND EMPTY ROOM.

NOTHING MOVED IN THERE.

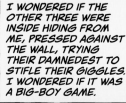
I WONDERED IF THE OTHER THREE WERE INSIDE HIDING FROM ME, PRESSED AGAINST THE WALL, TRYING THEIR DAMNEDEST TO STIFLE THEIR GIGGLES. I WONDERED IF IT WAS A BIG-BOY GAME.

I DIDN'T KNOW. I COULDN'T TELL.

I STOOD THERE IN THE COURTYARD OF THE PLAYHOUSE, WHILE THE SKY GOT DARKER, JUST WAITING.

THE MOON ROSE AFTER A WHILE, A BIG AUTUMN MOON THE COLOUR OF HONEY.

AND THEN, AFTER A WHILE, THE DOOR OPENED.

NOTHING CAME OUT.

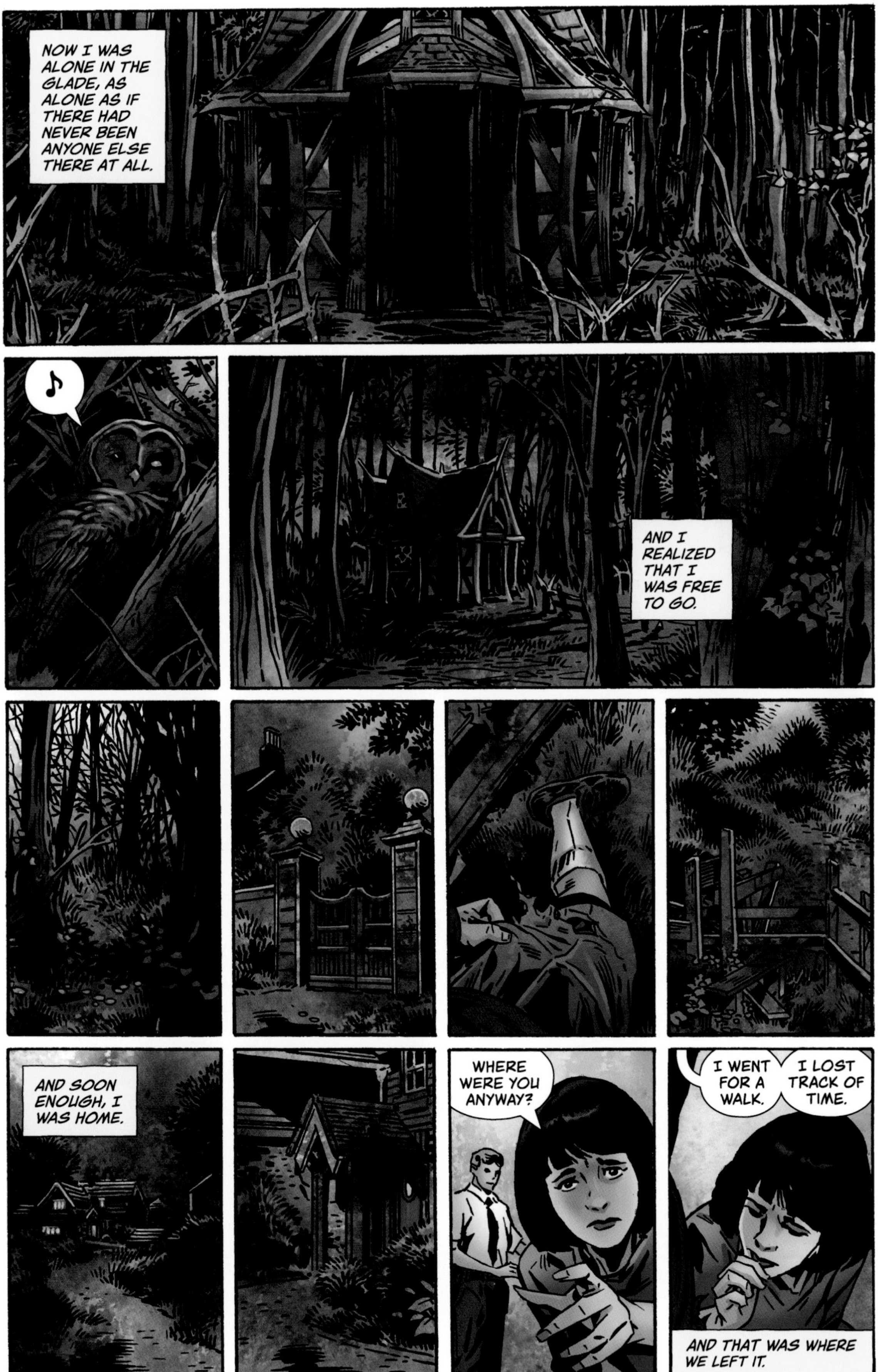
NOW I WAS ALONE IN THE GLADE, AS ALONE AS IF THERE HAD NEVER BEEN ANYONE ELSE THERE AT ALL.
♪
AND I REALIZED THAT I WAS FREE TO GO.
AND SOON ENOUGH, I WAS HOME.
WHERE WERE YOU ANYWAY?
I WENT FOR A WALK.
I LOST TRACK OF TIME.
AND THAT WAS WHERE WE LEFT IT.

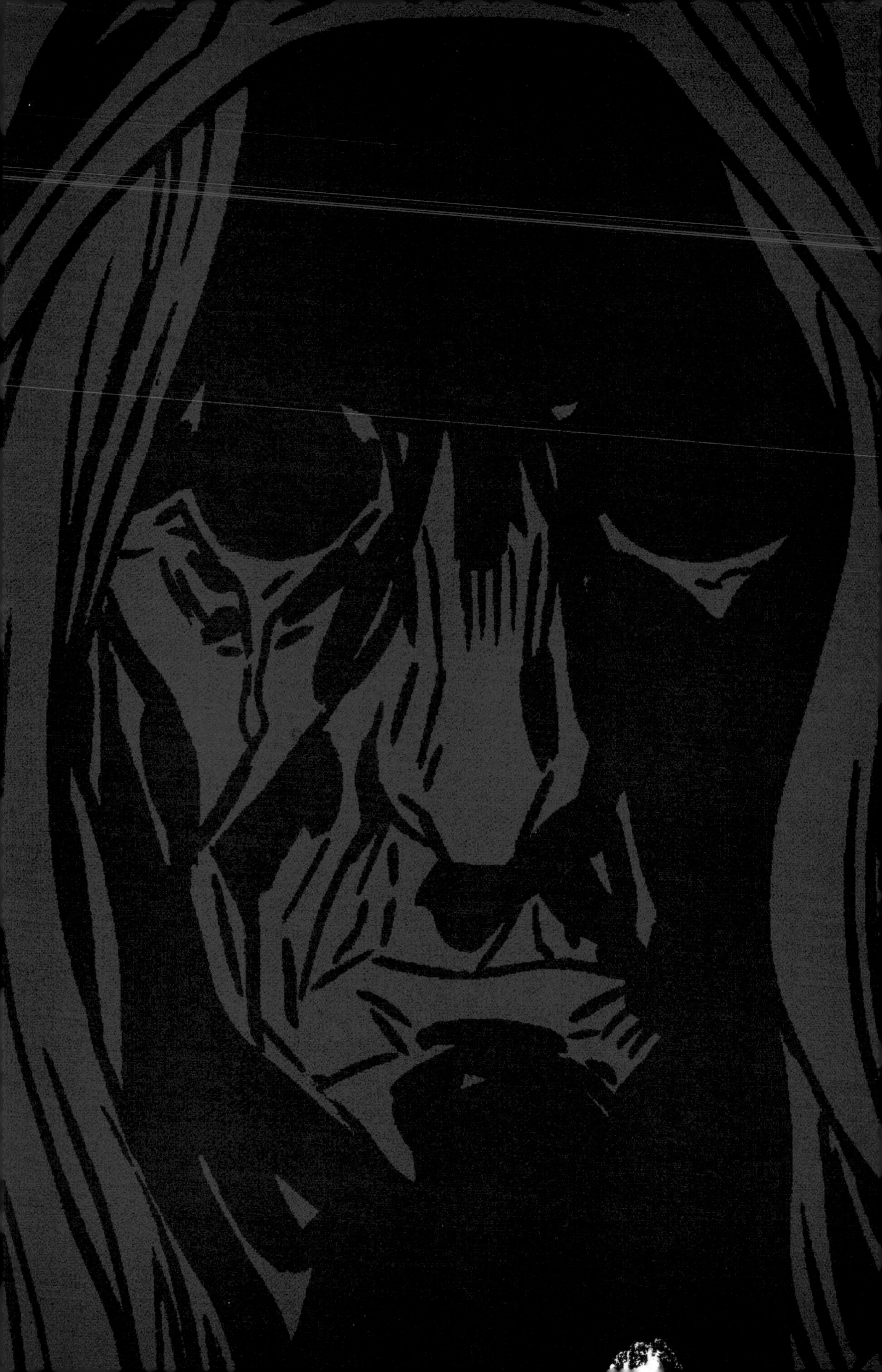

EPILOGUE

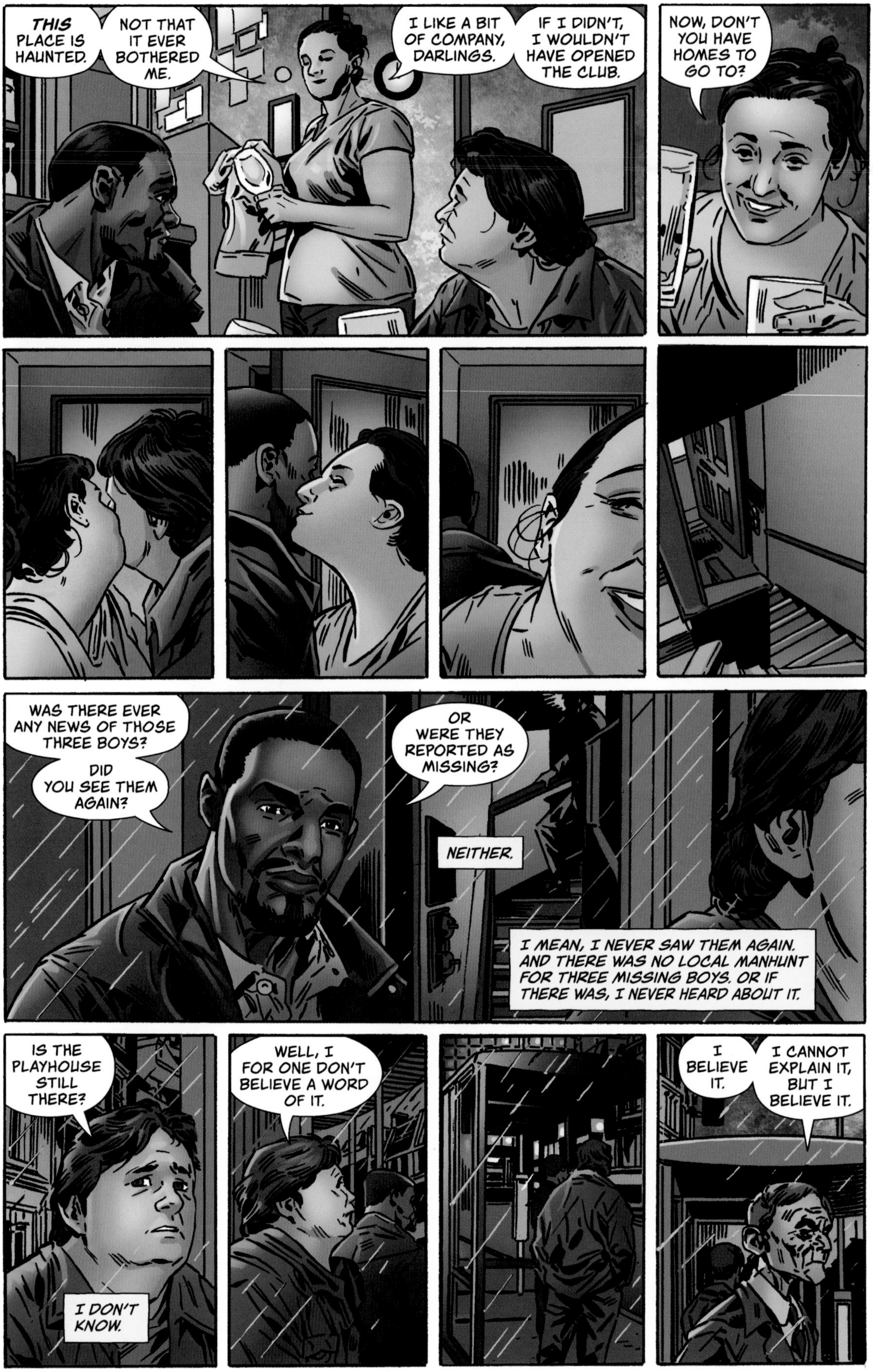
THIS PLACE IS HAUNTED.
NOT THAT IT EVER BOTHERED ME.
I LIKE A BIT OF COMPANY, DARLINGS.
IF I DIDN'T, I WOULDN'T HAVE OPENED THE CLUB.
NOW, DON'T YOU HAVE HOMES TO GO TO?
WAS THERE EVER ANY NEWS OF THOSE THREE BOYS?
DID YOU SEE THEM AGAIN?
OR WERE THEY REPORTED AS MISSING?
NEITHER.
I MEAN, I NEVER SAW THEM AGAIN. AND THERE WAS NO LOCAL MANHUNT FOR THREE MISSING BOYS. OR IF THERE WAS, I NEVER HEARD ABOUT IT.
IS THE PLAYHOUSE STILL THERE?
I DON'T KNOW.
WELL, I FOR ONE DON'T BELIEVE A WORD OF IT.
I BELIEVE IT.
I CANNOT EXPLAIN IT, BUT I BELIEVE IT.

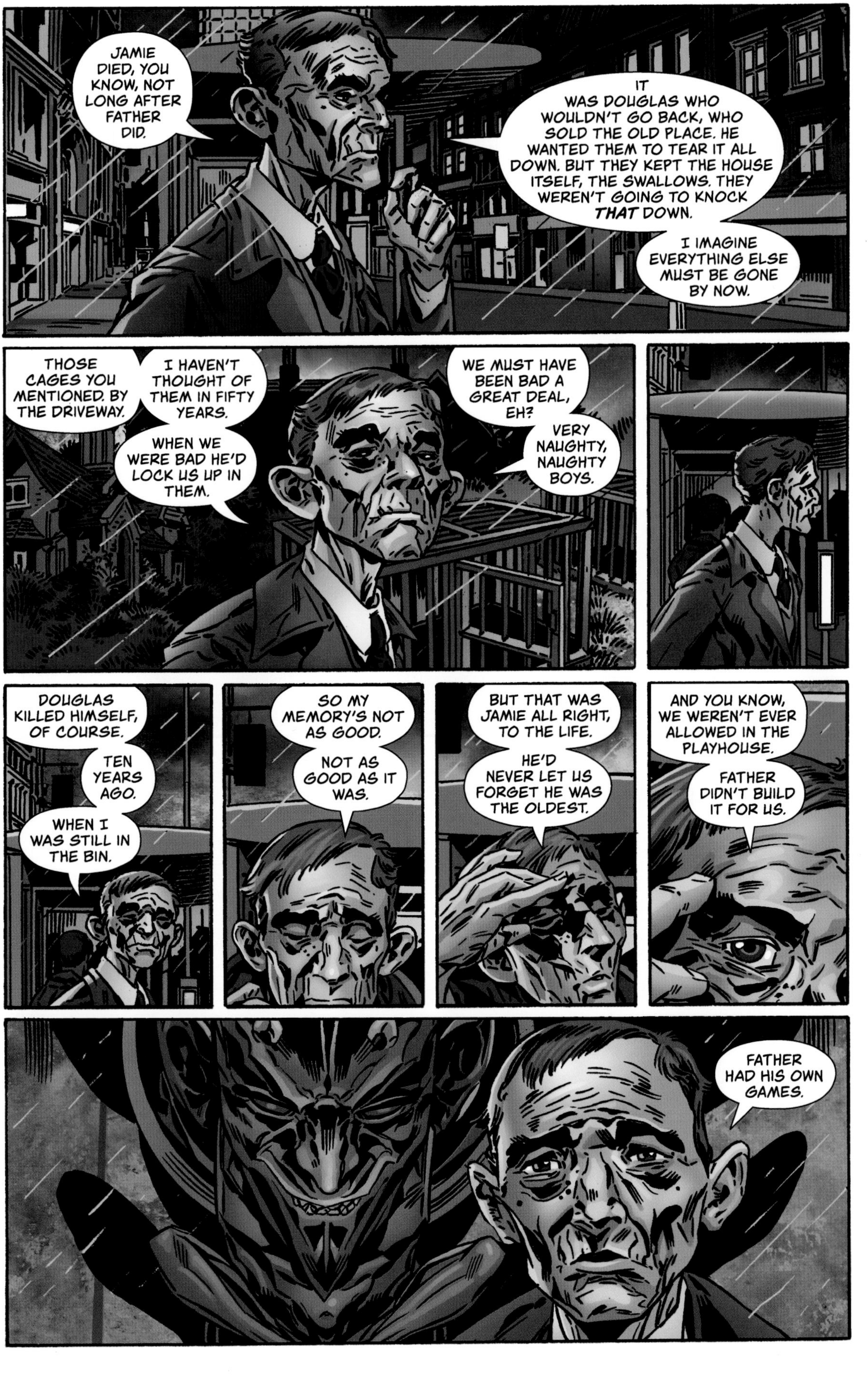
JAMIE DIED, YOU KNOW, NOT LONG AFTER FATHER DID.
IT WAS DOUGLAS WHO WOULDN'T GO BACK, WHO SOLD THE OLD PLACE. HE WANTED THEM TO TEAR IT ALL DOWN. BUT THEY KEPT THE HOUSE ITSELF, THE SWALLOWS. THEY WEREN'T GOING TO KNOCK *THAT* DOWN.
I IMAGINE EVERYTHING ELSE MUST BE GONE BY NOW.
THOSE CAGES YOU MENTIONED. BY THE DRIVEWAY.
I HAVEN'T THOUGHT OF THEM IN FIFTY YEARS.
WHEN WE WERE BAD HE'D LOCK US UP IN THEM.
WE MUST HAVE BEEN BAD A GREAT DEAL, EH?
VERY NAUGHTY, NAUGHTY BOYS.
DOUGLAS KILLED HIMSELF, OF COURSE.
TEN YEARS AGO.
WHEN I WAS STILL IN THE BIN.
SO MY MEMORY'S NOT AS GOOD.
NOT AS GOOD AS IT WAS.
BUT THAT WAS JAMIE ALL RIGHT, TO THE LIFE.
HE'D NEVER LET US FORGET HE WAS THE OLDEST.
AND YOU KNOW, WE WEREN'T EVER ALLOWED IN THE PLAYHOUSE.
FATHER DIDN'T BUILD IT FOR US.
FATHER HAD HIS OWN GAMES.

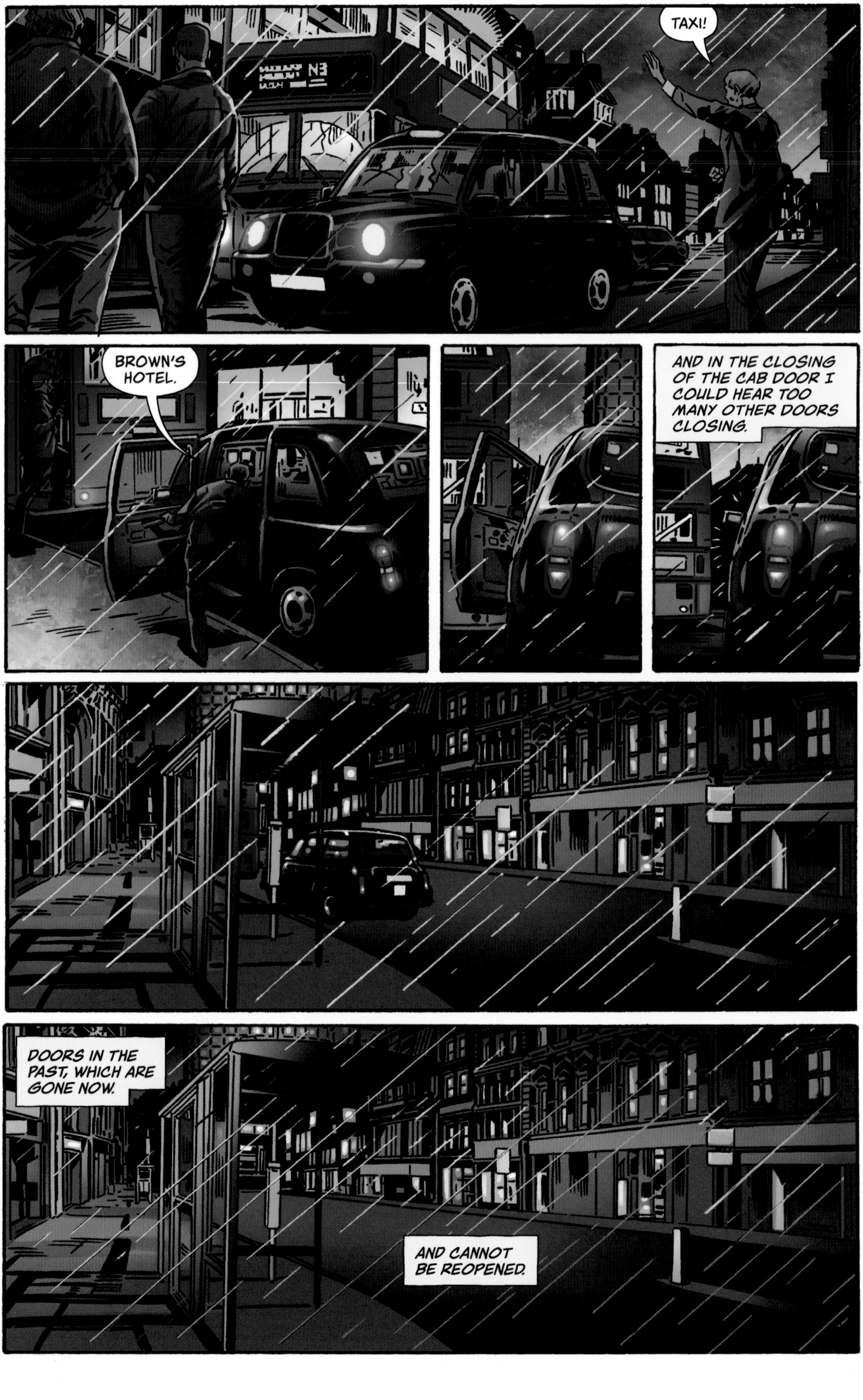
TAXI!
BROWN'S HOTEL.
AND IN THE CLOSING OF THE CAB DOOR I COULD HEAR TOO MANY OTHER DOORS CLOSING.
DOORS IN THE PAST, WHICH ARE GONE NOW.
AND CANNOT BE REOPENED.

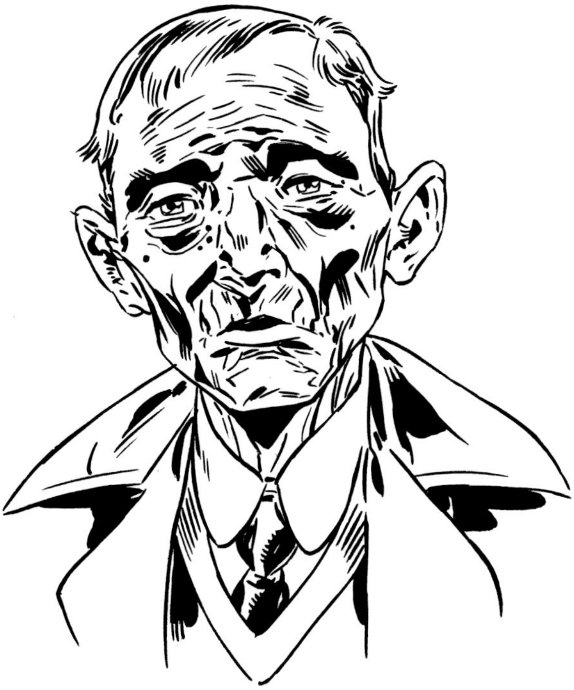

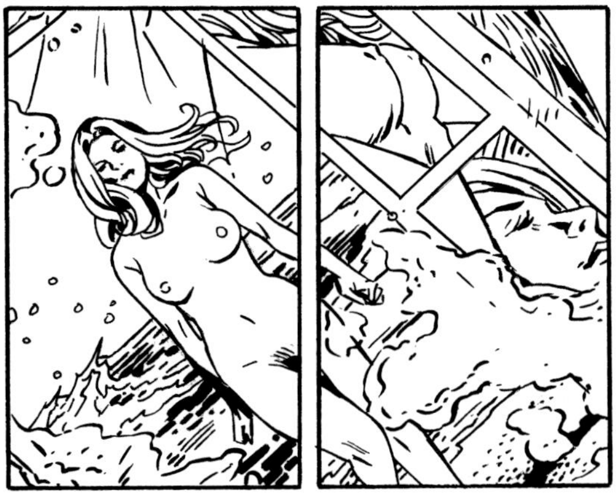

SKETCHBOOK

Notes by Mark Buckingham

TOP LEFT: A preproduction drawing of the old version of Simon from "Closing Time", and my favorite image of that character.

TOP RIGHT: Unused panels of Charlotte, originally drawn for story page 36, until I reread the script and realized the beach scene came two pages later. Silly me.

RIGHT & BOTTOM: A set of drawings of Eddie for "Feeders And Eaters", which were then worked into the final artwork.

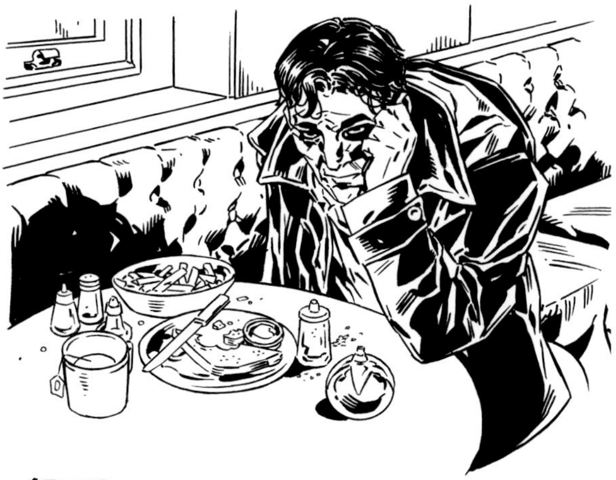

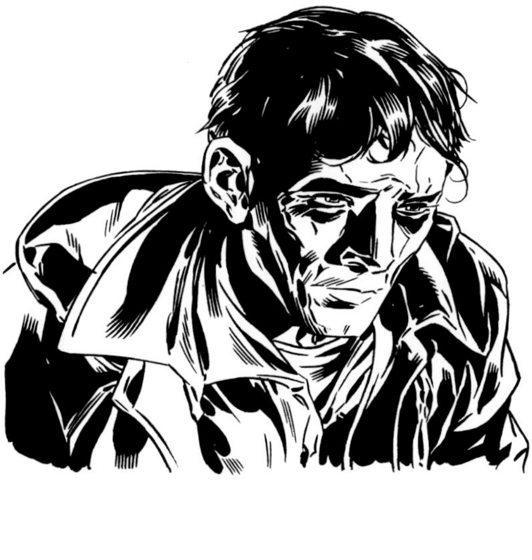

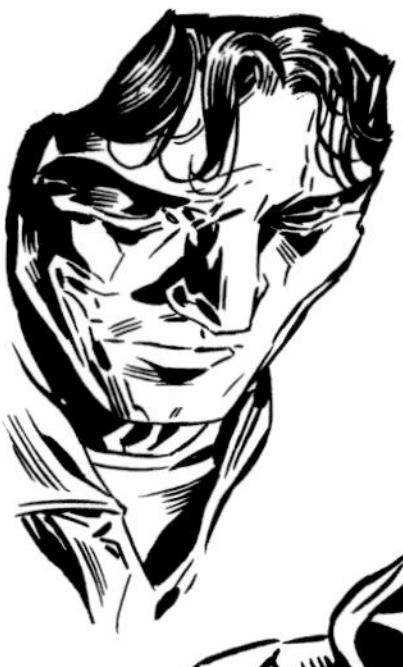

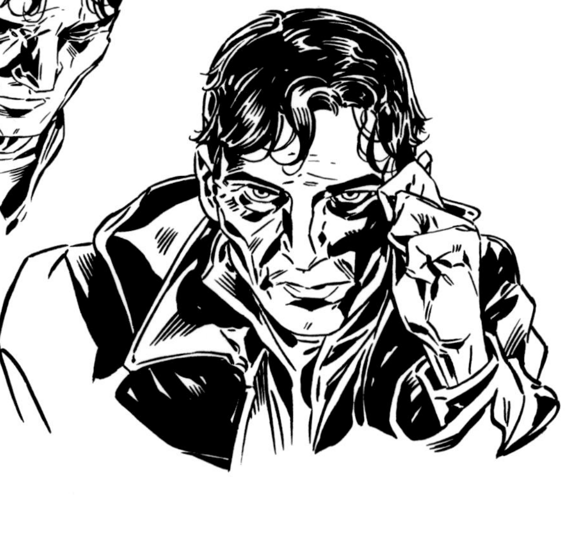

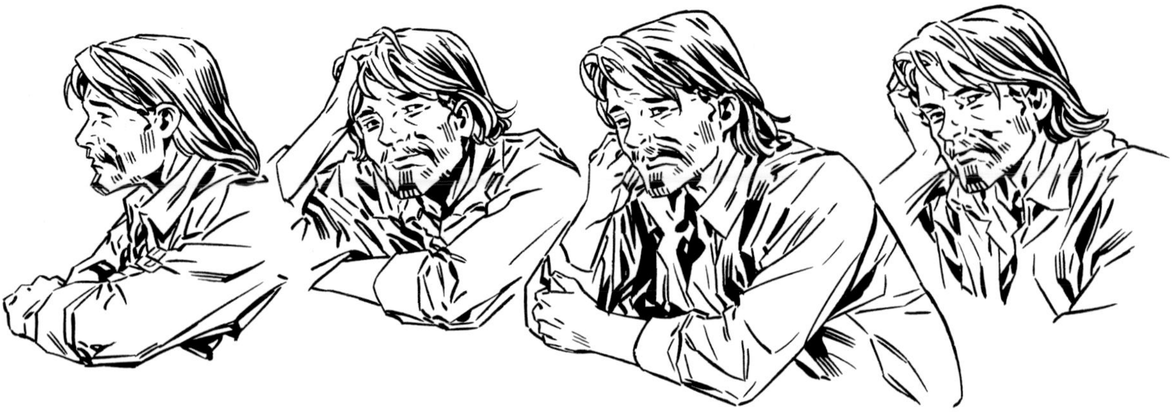

TOP: The photographer from "Looking For The Girl", in a set of drawings that again were incorporated into the final art.

MIDDLE: More images of the old man for the epilogue.

BOTTOM: Unused Charlotte art. An alternate panel for story page 38.

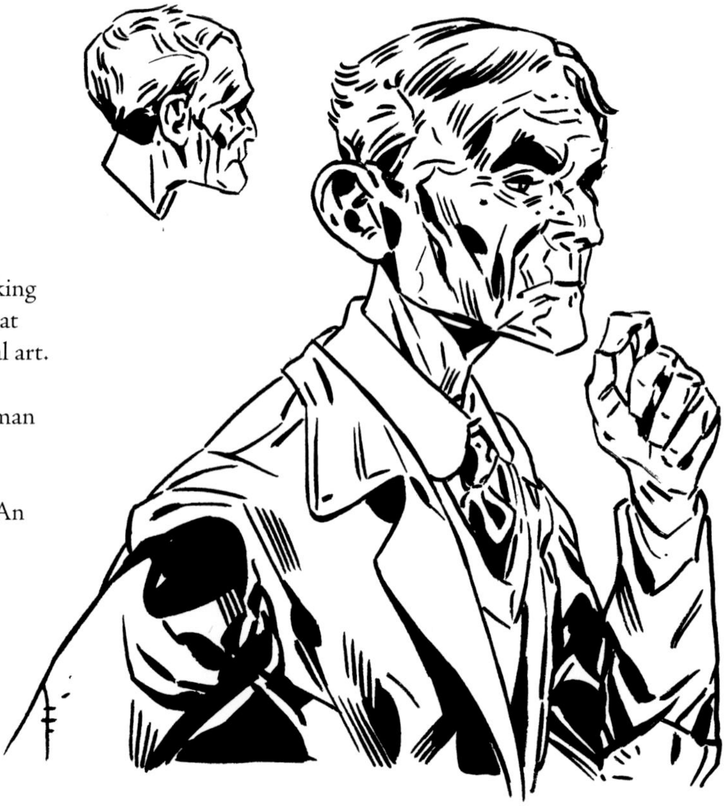

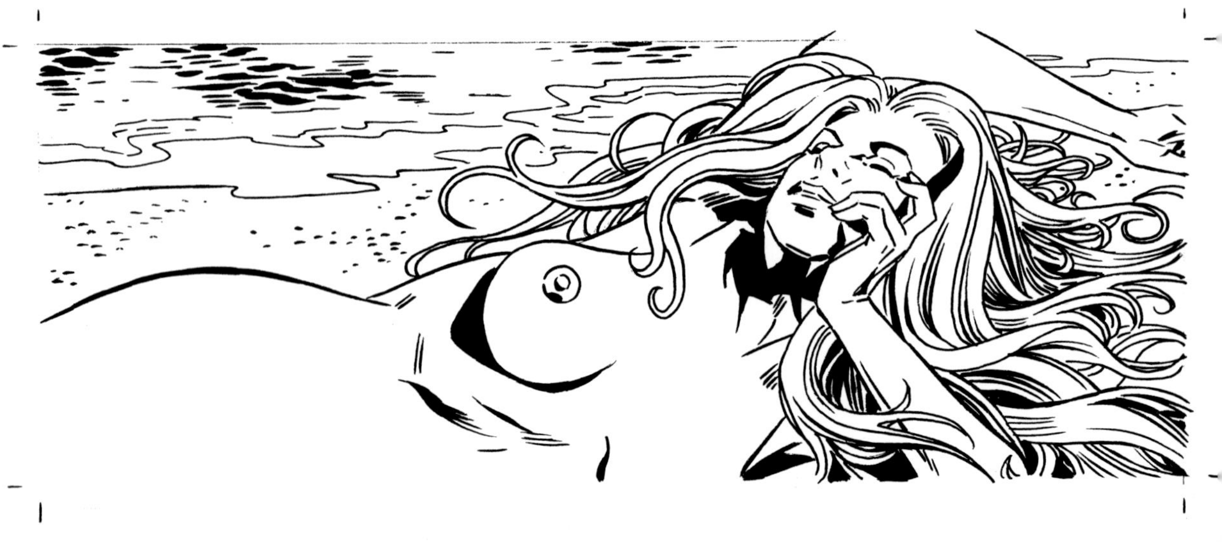

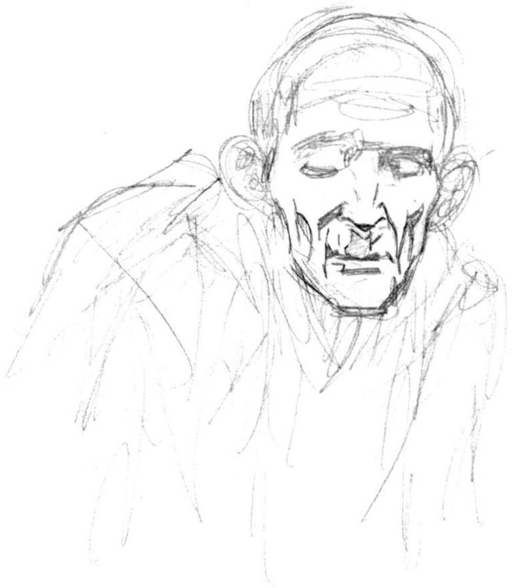

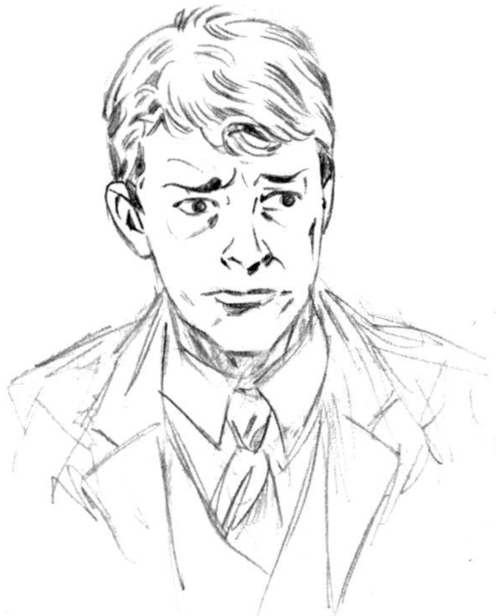

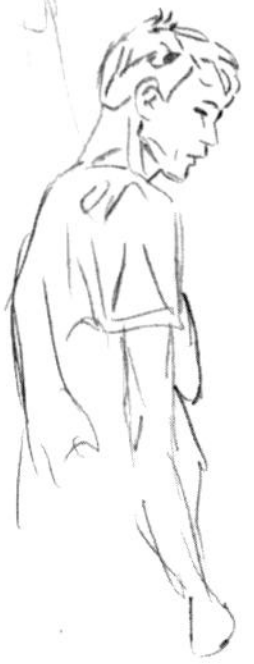

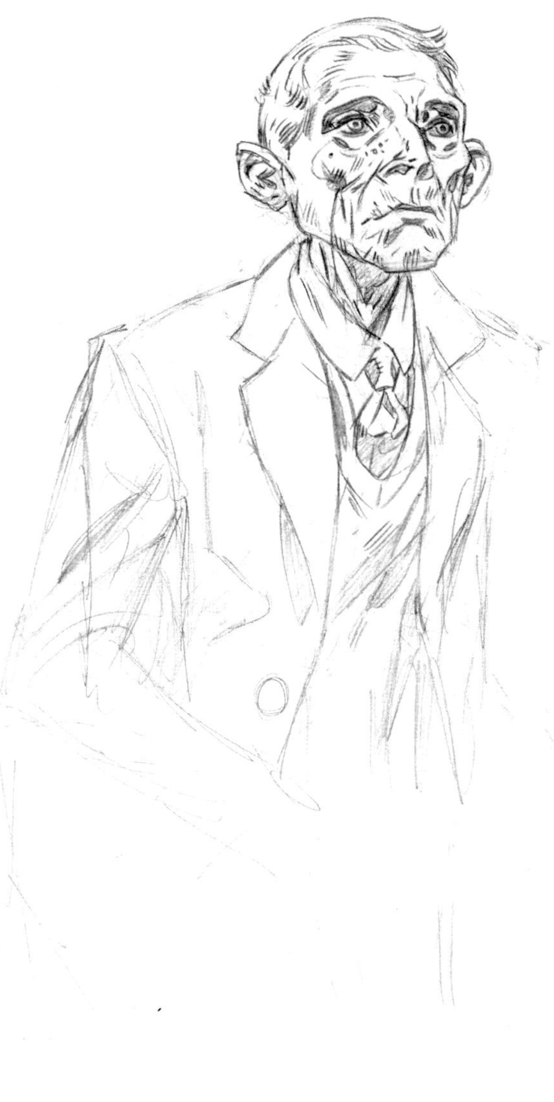

Character design pencil sketches for the two Simons in the *Likely Stories*.

BOTTOM RIGHT: My initial design for the evil imp door knocker in "Closing Time".

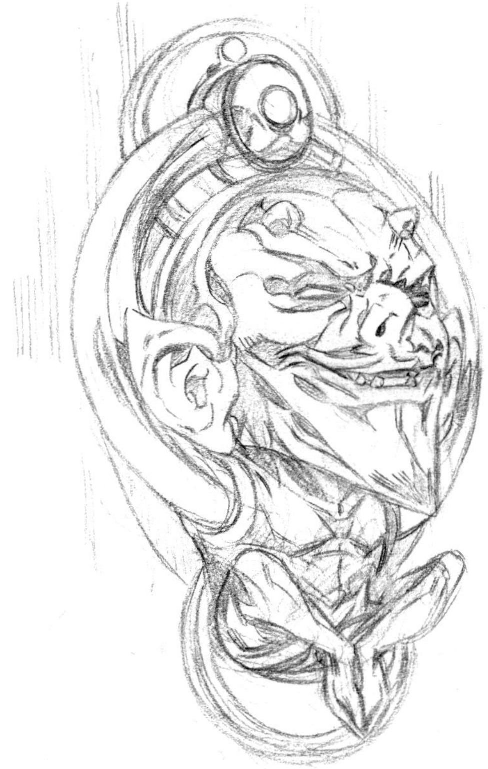

MORE TITLES FROM

THE NEIL GAIMAN LIBRARY

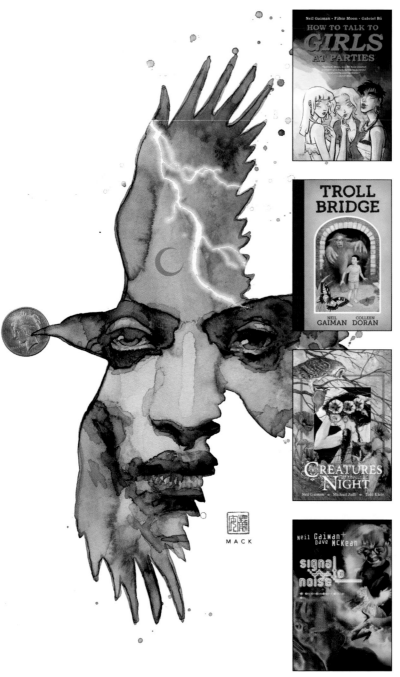

MACK